EVERYDAY WONDERS

Stories of God's Providence

V. REV. MICHAEL J. OLEKSA

ANCIENT FAITH PUBLISHING
CHESTERTON, INDIANA

Everyday Wonders: Stories of God's Providence
Copyright © 2018 Michael J. Oleksa

All rights reserved. No part of this publication may be reproduced by any means, electronic, mechanical, photocopying, recording, scanning, or otherwise, without the prior written permission of the publisher.

Published by:
 Ancient Faith Publishing
 A Division of Ancient Faith Ministries
 P.O. Box 748
 Chesterton, IN 46304

Unless otherwise noted, Scripture quotations are taken from the New King James Version, © 1979, 1980, 1982 by Thomas Nelson, Inc. Used by permission.

ISBN: 978-1-944967-35-2

30 29 28 27 26 25 24 23 22 21   17 16 15 14 13 12 11 10 9 8 7 6 5 4 3 2

Contents

Preface	5
ONE: North to Alaska	7
TWO: Holy Copters	17
THREE: Real People	25
FOUR: World War II and the ATG	41
FIVE: Lost and Found	51
SIX: Receiving My ThD	57
SEVEN: Roots Trips: 1988, 1999, 2014	65
EIGHT: Suceava	77
NINE: Time Out!	87
TEN: Robbed!	103
ELEVEN: Matushka Olga Michael	119
TWELVE: The Blessings of Theophany	131

For my grandson, Nicholas,
and my granddaughter, Aurelia

Preface

THE STORIES AND ESSAYS that are included in this little volume were written over many years and for many different audiences. They witness to life experiences that are too amazing to be considered coincidences but certainly not so astounding as to be considered miracles. They are ordinary events which a cynical or secular person might dismiss as accidental, but which a believer would probably attribute to God. Despite all the academic debates about "proving" God's existence and His interest and care for us in our daily lives, I see no logical or irrefutable "proof" better than everyday experience. For those who know and love God, He is "everywhere present and filling all things." He is the source of all life, so that we see Him in every living thing, in plants and animals, and most certainly in each other. "Show me God," the doubter might demand, "and I will believe." The believer must retort, "Show me what is not God!"

The Greek Fathers teach that God not only created the

EVERYDAY WONDERS

world, however many billions of years ago, but He sustains it from one moment to the next. The world is created in this moment, and then again in this moment, and then, amazingly, in this moment as well. The cosmos speaks of God as its Source, Creator, Sustainer, Goal, and Purpose.

Certainly there are those who might want to challenge this experience of the visible world, the created universe, but their logical, rational arguments will never decisively undermine the faith of those whose lives are filled with Everyday Wonders.

—Archpriest Michael Oleksa

✠ ONE ✠

North to Alaska

IN THIRD GRADE I learned the lyrics to a Johnny Horton song called "North to Alaska," along with his ballad about the Battle of New Orleans. The British, if I recall, ran down to the Gulf of Mexico, but when it came to Alaska, "the rush was on." These, for me, turned out to be prophetic words.

Ever since I learned that there were Orthodox Christians who were also Alaska Natives, I was secretly determined to go there. Here my two greatest lifelong interests, Native Americans and Orthodoxy, were united in one place, and I didn't even need a passport to get there! This was a phenomenon I sincerely wanted to experience and explore.

When I heard that one of the first missionaries from Russia to Alaska, Father Herman, was being glorified as a saint in August 1970, I started looking for a way to work somewhere in the state so I could participate in that celebration. This would be a once-in-a-lifetime event. I wrote letters to various chambers of commerce and offered my services. The few replies I received were all polite but firm rejections. There was a recession in progress. The State of Alaska had set up an information booth in the Seattle-Tacoma airport to discourage job-seekers from coming to Alaska. The prospects of finding employment there were very poor indeed.

Then another amazing scenario began to unfold. A recent college graduate who had enlisted in Volunteers in Service to America (VISTA) had been chosen to serve in Fairbanks, Alaska, that year, but his assignment had not panned out. On his way home, he had stopped to visit Sitka, the former Russian capital of Alaska, and had been recruited to stay on for the year, assisting with the youth program at St. Michael's Cathedral and with the religious education classes at the Bureau of Indian Affairs (BIA) secondary boarding school.

Decades earlier, an evangelical missionary had come to Old Harbor, the village on Kodiak Island where the first Orthodox church in the new world had been founded in 1784. She had established herself as a kindergarten teacher in the village and opened her house to children interested in both treats and Sunday school instruction. Over the years, she had influenced many with her sectarian ideas and was ready to "baptize" several of them, now as adults, into her church, separating them from their Orthodox heritage and roots and creating a schism in the community. Unhappy as their Orthodox relatives were about the situation, they could not prevent her colleagues from coming on Good Friday 1964 to perform the ceremony that would divide the village religiously forever. But the shocks and jolts of the largest earthquake to rock North America interrupted and cancelled those plans.

The epicenter of the quake was several hundred miles northeast of Kodiak, but the tsunami it generated came sweeping across the Gulf of Alaska with tremendous force and speed. The village of Chenega, much closer to the center of the catastrophe, was completely destroyed, and many of its citizens, including small children running from the wave, were taken by the sea. The wave hit Seward, Kodiak, Kaguyak, Afognak, Ouzinkie, and Old Harbor, as well as Crescent City, California, thousands of miles to the south. Streets in Anchorage collapsed. The continent had not experienced a disaster like this in centuries.

Old Harbor residents fled up the hill immediately behind their homes, high enough above sea level to guarantee their personal safety—and to provide an unobstructed view of what was about to happen to the homes. First, the fjord in front of the town went dry, exposing the ocean floor, which none of them had ever expected to see in their lives. As the ocean water came rushing back, it devastated one side of the village, twisting the BIA school off its foundations and washing many of their houses out to sea. The wave returned from the opposite direction and headed straight for Three Saints Church.

Someone in the crowd yelled, "Our church is going to go!"

A young man blurted out, "No! The cross is holding it down!"

The wave incredibly and inexplicably split, went around the church, leaving it unscathed, rose up the hill to take even the highest structures in the town, and receded. The last wave took the rest of the homes. All that remained of the village was the school, knocked off its concrete foundations, and the wooden, unanchored Three Saints Orthodox Church, sitting flat on the beach, miraculously preserved. Later, when residents were able to make their way to the church, they found the interior undisturbed. Nothing, not even a candle, had fallen.

After the villagers had been evacuated to Anchorage, they discussed whether to return to the same site. Hadn't there been other tsunamis in the past? Maybe they should consider relocating the village. No, the elders decided. God had saved their church. He wanted them to stay there. There would be a new beginning.

Those potentially divisive baptisms were never rescheduled. When the kindergarten-teacher/missionary returned to gather her belongings, there was an aftershock. She turned to the villagers and barked, "You can't blame me for that one!" She never came back.

The town required some time to rebuild, the survivors living in tents while new homes arose along Sitkalidak Straits. A new generation assumed leadership, led by the young man who had prophesied about the cross and the church. He became mayor and served his community for the next twenty-seven years. Sven Haakanson, the son of a Danish father and an Alutiiq mother, wrote to the bishop in Sitka to ask for a pastor for Old Harbor.

The reply came, "How can I send you a priest when there is no house for him and his family?"

Sven organized the town to provide a small cottage, connected its electricity and plumbing, and replied, "We have a house. Please send us a priest."

The bishop responded, "How can I send you a priest when you have no means of supporting him, no funds for a stipend? How can he survive with no regular income?"

Sven had the fishermen of the village sign a request that a certain amount be paid to the church from their annual checks, issued by Columbia Wards Fisheries, their cannery. "We have money for a salary now deposited in the bank. Please send us a priest."

At this point the bishop had to be completely honest. "Well, I'd be glad to send you a priest if I had one available. The truth is, I have no one to send!"

Sven considered the options. There was no one ordained and waiting to be assigned, but wasn't there a seminary somewhere? If they couldn't find someone who was already ordained, maybe they could recruit someone who soon would be. He drafted another letter to the bishop requesting a seminarian.

The bishop had graduated over a decade earlier and was no longer personally familiar with anyone enrolled at St. Vladimir's Seminary in New York. But that VISTA volunteer I mentioned earlier, resident in his house that year, had a cousin there. He offered to forward the letter to him and invite him to come to Alaska.

This cousin was an inveterate New York City guy. I had a roommate once who was of the same mindset. These people believe that The City, as they call it, is the only place on the planet worth living in. The sun rises on the East River and sets on the Hudson. The West is New Jersey, and they never go there. If Ohio was too far to venture, the Pacific Northwest was unimaginable.

My room in the dorm was not thirty yards from his. But he had no idea I'd been trying to find a way to get to Kodiak. He asked his roommates, both of whom had prior commitments to return to their home states. He knocked on every door on that floor and finally came to mine. His words still echo:

"You might think this is crazy, Mike, but would you by any chance be interested in going to Alaska this summer?"

I almost fell off my chair!

Two weeks later I was flying across North America to

Seattle, and then on a direct flight on Western Airlines to Kodiak. Father Makarios Targonsky welcomed me to the city and to his home, where I had the pleasure of meeting his Palestinian wife and their five adopted Alutiiq children. I stayed with him a few days, until he could find time to accompany me on one of the most exciting adventures of my life.

We boarded an amazing flying machine called a Grumman Goose. The plane had both wheels and pontoons, as well as two huge propellers. There might have been, potentially, room for more passengers, but most of the hull was filled with freight. The plane was aptly named—it waddled like a goose and plopped itself into the ocean, then started one engine, throwing gallons of seawater against the windows on one side of the plane. It felt like we were in a submarine. Then the second engine started, with the same watery result, as the Goose made its way out into the harbor. Trying with all its might to gain speed, it amazingly rose into the air. It could fly after all, but with a takeoff similar to that of the many sea parrots (or puffins) that thrive in this region.

We flew over magnificent peaks and beautiful bays bearing exotic Alutiiq names. The scenery reminded me of Greece, where I'd visited two summers before. The water and sky were different shades of blue, the vegetation was sprouting and darkening in fifty shades of green, and a ribbon of white snow still crowned the peaks of the interior. I was in love with this land, this place, already.

EVERYDAY WONDERS

Our landing was equally extraordinary. The giant puffin belly-flopped onto the North Pacific Ocean, waddled ashore, and discharged its passengers onto the rocky beach. Several dozen village children surrounded the plane, waiting for their new teacher to emerge.

I don't think I was disappointed, but I was certainly surprised to meet these kids. They all spoke English. They all wore normal, store-bought American clothes. They ate hamburgers and pizza, played basketball, chewed bubble gum—like American kids anywhere. At first, it didn't seem that cultural or linguistic problems were going to interfere with our relationships. These children were like any others in the US, I erroneously concluded. But I had arrived in a town like no other on earth, the place where the written history of Alaska began—thanks to one VISTA volunteer whose assignment in Fairbanks had fallen through, his cousin who was not willing to venture west of the Hudson River, and, less directly, one huge earthquake and tidal wave.

My assignment was to run Aleut School. Since I had been recruited from an Orthodox seminary, I assumed this entailed mostly religious education, which of course it did. However, before I departed at the end of August to return to New York for my second year of theological studies, I had my students recite and perform a few hymns they had learned in Alutiiq, Church Slavonic, and English. At the conclusion of our little program, several village elders approached me and commented, "We're so happy, Michael, that you finally got it right."

Only then did I realize that Aleut School entailed more than Bible study or liturgical singing. The community was determined to retain their tradition of reading, writing, and worshiping in their ancestral languages—Alutiiq, Russian, and now English. This was their heritage, and they sought the support of the Church to maintain and transmit it. I had come North to Alaska, which was for me now North to the Future, as our license plates proclaim. I would spend the rest of my life and nearly all my priestly ministry learning from, as well as serving, these wonderful, amazing Alaska Native people.

✠ TWO ✠

Holy Copters

THE MONK HERMAN was one of the original missionaries who traversed the entire Russian Empire—8,000 miles, mostly on foot—to the Pacific coast and sailed to America, arriving on Kodiak Island on September 24, 1794. Father Herman had been living a monastic life since his teen years and was the senior member of the missionary delegation that Gregory Shelikov, head of the Russian-American Company, recruited at Valaam Monastery.

Arriving at St. Paul Harbor, the monks were shocked at the abusive treatment to which the Sugpiaq people of the island were being subjected. The company's chief manager, Alexander Baranov, was dismayed at the arrival of the clergy, knowing they would soon become whistle-blowers on his violent but highly profitable operation. Within months, Father

Herman was writing to Shelikov, complaining of Baranov's oppressive methods of extorting furs from the local population.

The monastic delegation was ill fated. Some monks perished at sea, another was martyred on the Alaskan mainland with his Athabaskan (Tanaina) Indian guide, and others, discouraged by the company's ill treatment of them and the Native people, returned to Russia. Within a decade, Herman was the sole surviving missionary.

But he barely survived. Reports indicate that there were plots to kill him afoot in Kodiak town, so for the sake of peace and security, Herman relocated to nearby Elovoi or Spruce Island. He dug himself a cave, as was the ancient practice of Orthodox monks since the appearance of Christian monasticism in the Egyptian desert. (Anthony the Great fled to the wilderness, the region the Bible had declared to be the devils' land, the place where the demons go when they are cast out. There, in this enemy-occupied territory, Anthony, and later his disciples, settled as a liberating, invading force, proclaiming and celebrating Christ's victory over evil, sin, darkness, and death itself.)

So Herman "invaded" Spruce Island in the name of the living God, eventually building a chapel and, later, an orphanage there. He spent his days in prayer and in cultivating the soil, feeding the children whom he'd brought there after a horrible smallpox epidemic took many of their parents and elders. He continued to protest the illegal policies of the

Russian-American Company throughout his life, and the Aleuts loved him for his heroic defense of their culture and their civil rights. They built a chapel over his grave in 1894 to mark the centennial of his arrival, and this became a pilgrimage site over the next several decades. Miracles of healing regularly occurred there. Even non-Orthodox locals could not deny that there was a source of sacred healing power emanating from his gravesite and the holy spring that flowed nearby.

In 1969, the Holy Synod decided to set aside a day on the calendar to celebrate the holy life of the Monk Herman: August 9. Since no one lived at Monk's Lagoon, where he was buried, and reaching there would be difficult for the thousands of people who would now want to pray at his tomb, it was decided to move his coffin to Holy Resurrection Church, where his relics would be much more accessible. The priest at Holy Resurrection was Father Makarios, who took me for that memorable ride in the Grumman Goose when I first came to Alaska. It became his task to transfer the holy remains to Kodiak.

There is no dock on that part of Spruce Island where a boat could anchor. There is no airport at which a plane could land. The nearest village, Ouzinkie, lies at the western end of the island, eight miles away. The coffin had been rebuilt and covered with a shroud by Father Gerassim Schmaltz, a Russian monk who had lived on Mount Athos before coming to attend to the holy bones of the Venerable Monk Herman.

EVERYDAY WONDERS

He had enshrined his body in a new coffin and placed it in the nave of the memorial chapel that had been built there by the Aleut faithful in 1894. But how was Father Makarios to get it to the mainland?

Providentially, at exactly that time, the local "bush" or air taxi company acquired a small helicopter—the perfect vehicle for transporting the coffin to the city, which was not more than ten miles away as the eagle flies. Having engaged them to fly to Monk's Lagoon, Father Makarios was able to find a few volunteers to assist him in carrying the coffin to the rocky beach and loading it onto the helicopter. The icon painted for the glorification of Saint Herman of Alaska includes about twenty scenes from his life and also his canonization. This is perhaps the only iconographic depiction of a helicopter ever made.

Forty-four years later, Father Makarios fell asleep in the Lord in the city of Kenai. I had been blessed to serve at the services glorifying Saint Herman that summer, lodging in the basement of his house during the festivities and enjoying his hospitality and amazing tenor voice. His specialty, his trademark song, was *"Vechernii Zvon"* ("Evening Bells"). He sang this song at every wedding banquet, baptismal party, clergy dinner, or even funeral meal, whenever someone requested it.

I had enjoyed visiting with his wife, an Orthodox woman from the Holy City of Jerusalem, and used to practice my college Arabic with her in a home where visitors most often spoke Russian. It was our little joke that if they were going to speak in Russian, which at that time neither of us understood, we could have our own conversation in Arabic. Matushka Yvette and I were always close friends.

In fact, in 1971, not long after the feast of St. Herman, she saved my life.

That summer, my second in Alaska, I had spent three months in *Lingit Aani*, the Land of Tlingit, the southeast panhandle of Alaska along the Canadian border. Based in Sitka, I traveled on the Alaska Marine Highway, the state-subsidized ferry system, to the villages of Angoon and Hoonah, where I was adopted into the *Kaagwaantaan* clan, on the Eagle "side" or moiety of the Tlingit Nation. My name, *Kuxwoos.gaax*, means "call back." It refers to the echo of the wolf's cry, but it was given to me because the elders hoped I would call the community back to God.

I had spent the week after the Feast of St. Herman with my friends at Old Harbor. I was on my way to the Kodiak airport to fly on to Sitka, fetch my belongings, and return, probably forever, to the East Coast. But as I walked up Mission Road toward the parish rectory, I was shocked to see that its exterior walls were painted in stripes. The original pale green color was punctuated with long strokes of dark green, and the house looked, well, ridiculous. I wanted to say farewell to Matushka Yvette and Father Makarios, but when I entered, she was in a terrible state.

"What happened to your house?" I asked in amazement.

"There were two students painting it, and one of them got news that his sister was getting married this weekend, so they dropped everything and flew back to New York!"

"And they just left your house in this zebra design?"

"Yes! And you know here in Kodiak, even during the summer, we have only a few warm, sunny days. If the house is not painted soon, who knows how long it will remain like this, till we have appropriate painting weather!"

"Oh, I'm sorry, Matushka. I'd be glad to help, but my flight to Sitka departs in an hour. I have to hurry to the airport!"

"No! You're the only one who is available. The sun is shining! It's a perfect day to paint the house—at least the striped front of it. Please finish at least the west side of the building. There are flights to Anchorage and on to Sitka every day, and you can change your reservation by phone. Please! Michael!"

The paint cans, brushes, and ladders were right where the previous painters had left them a few hours earlier, and I got immediately to work. I hoped to complete at least one coat on the green zebra wall, catch a later jet to Anchorage, and connect to Sitka. But the wall needed two coats, and the job took the rest of that long summer day. By nine PM, however, the front of the house looked new and normal again.

"I had better call to tell the bishop not to expect me this evening," I said to Matushka. "He'll be going to the Sitka airport soon, awaiting my arrival."

"Certainly! Please use the phone in the kitchen," she replied.

I dialed the home number of the bishop's residence in Sitka and heard His Grace answer.

"Hello, Your Grace! Please give me your blessing!"

"May the Lord God bless you . . . Michael! Michael! Is that you?"

"Yes, Your Grace. I'm sorry I didn't call earlier, but I won't be arriving in Sitka this evening after all."

"Oh, thank God you're alive!"

"Alive? Of course I'm alive. Why wouldn't I be alive?"

"The news just arrived here from Juneau. The flight coming in from Anchorage, the plane you were scheduled to be aboard, crashed into the mountain. They fear there are no survivors. I was looking in your room for your parents' telephone number just now, wanting them to hear from me first. I've been so distraught for the last hour, thinking you were on that jet! We've all been crying!"

Had I insisted on my own agenda and left the Kodiak house in its silly stripes, I would probably not be alive today. Always do what a matushka asks!

I was asked to speak about Father Makarios at his funeral. I reminded the family and friends gathered at Holy Assumption (Dormition) Orthodox Church in Kenai how Father Makarios had sung "Evening Bells" for decades and how much he was renowned for his beautiful tenor voice.

"Whenever we hear that folk song, we will remember him, won't we?" Tearfully, everyone agreed.

"And whenever I see a helicopter, I will think of him too." And I told the story of the transfer of St. Herman's relics to Kodiak.

At the conclusion of the services, we carried Father Makarios's coffin to the waiting hearse and prepared to drive the short distance to the parish cemetery. However, less than two hundred yards from the church, we were prevented from moving forward. A double-parked car blocked the road.

While several men went door to door in the neighborhood to find the owner of the car, the rest of the funeral procession—hundreds of mourners—stopped right where they were and stood in silence, patiently awaiting the removal of this obstacle that blocked our path.

From nowhere, we heard a rumbling noise, a thud-thud-thud, and a helicopter flew over us, buzzing the procession, as if to salute us. The entire crowd turned, looked at me, and burst into a spontaneous laugh. It is the only time in my four decades of priestly ministry that I recall a funeral party smiling so broadly, laughing so loudly.

As far as I know, there are no helicopters stationed at the Kenai airport. And if that car had not been there, we would have passed by quickly and missed that fly-over.

Nothing happens by accident. God is much more in charge than we know.

✠ THREE ✠

Real People

MY FATHER-IN-LAW was born into a traditional Yup'ik family who lived a semi-nomadic existence on the upper reaches of the Kwethluk River. They were hardly aware the outside world existed. They hunted, trapped, gathered, and fished the way they always had, subsisting off the land and waters. Their clothes were homemade from fur and leather, their tools fashioned from bone, wood, and stone. Their houses were semi-subterranean, dug several feet into the ground to let the wind sweep over them, rather than standing arrogantly upright to receive the full force of howling blizzards for six months of the year. The domed roofline of a traditional sod house bowed prayerfully to the ground, like an Orthodox monk making a prostration, submitting to rather than resisting the inevitable harsh realities of the world.

EVERYDAY WONDERS

Alaska teaches a person to go with the flow. You may have plans, but a hundred unforeseen forces can join to overthrow them. You want to travel, but it's too foggy, too windy, too cold, too rainy, too cloudy; the ice is too thin, the mud is too soft, the engine is broken, someone else is using it, no one cleaned it, shoveled it, prepared it. You're expecting a package, but the planes aren't flying, the postmaster is sick, there's a funeral today, the plane couldn't bring the mail because there were too many boxes, too many people, not enough room in the cargo bay, the pilot forgot it, a sled dog ate it. Burger King advertises, "Have it your way!" Alaska warns, "Don't bet on it!"

Southwestern Alaska is subject to floods as the winter ice breaks up and surges toward the Bering Sea each spring. If the ice jams at any point, a lake will form behind the ice-dam, causing widespread flooding in the region. I arrived there during the spring of 1972, and there was water, water everywhere. We traveled upriver to Kwethluk (Kuiggluk), a village named "Bad River" because its own tributary of the larger Kuskokwim changed channels regularly and made it difficult to navigate. There was so much water that the skiff we used was able to skim over the tops of the submerged trees.

The high school students who had invited me to visit their village took me out hunting and fishing with them. I had absolutely no experience in either, but they were very patient with me. One snowy May afternoon, we stopped to warm ourselves on the shores of a huge lake, entering a wall tent that was pitched there. It seemed the family who was camping there had left their home in the village, since it was surrounded by rising floodwaters, and made the best of the situation by going camping until the ice jam broke. A beautiful little two-year-old toddler ran from me in terror, fleeing to the welcoming arms of her auntie.

We were welcomed with a cup of hot tea, and I chatted with the young lady as she continued to calm her frightened niece. I did not know that loving aunt would, two years later, become my lovely wife. I met Xenia on the shores of that "lake," the place where she had been born three decades earlier during a similar spring flood.

When my high school students took me hunting that summer during the flood, they came home with about a dozen muskrats. I was staying with an elderly couple who spoke little English. I wanted to immerse myself in the language and culture, and they offered me that opportunity. So my friends brought all these muskrats to that house, a log cabin standing on the left bank of the Kwethluk River.

The lady of the house was delighted and immediately skinned and gutted the catch, putting the pelts on sticks and placing them behind the woodstove to dry. These would be part of someone's *atkuq* (parka) someday. The meat was placed in a large pot of boiling water. (I tease my Yup'ik wife that their cookbook has only one recipe: boil water, add ingredients, season to taste, serve when done. Presto! A Yup'ik supper.)

My hostess then set the table. She put spoons at each place setting, and then she brought a bucket of clean water into the house, soaked several washcloths in the water and wrung them out, and placed them down the middle of the table. I had never seen a dinner table prepared in this way, but I did not ask any questions. I was already learning that the culture preferred observation to conversation. Better to watch and keep quiet than to talk too much.

When the stew was ready, we were summoned to the table—myself, my friends, and a half-dozen other men. It was soup, as expected, but a different kind than I had ever eaten before. There was broth with carrots, rice, and onions, and then each guest had one muskrat—the entire animal, teeth, claws, belly. The critter had not been chopped up, and its entire body would obviously not fit onto a spoon. I was at a loss—how does one eat this?

Of course, all the other gentlemen at the table were familiar with this sort of meal and dipped directly into the bowl, removing the well-cooked meat from the carcass with their fingers. When the broth got a bit messy, the washcloths were available to tidy up a bit before resuming. *I can do this!* I thought to myself.

Of course, my high school mentors were not going to make this initiation into their culture easy. They had been to boarding school and suffered through their own crosscultural initiation into Anglo-American culture, but they had never witnessed a *kass'aaq* (white man) attempting to cross the cultural bridge from the other direction. They were going to enjoy this!

One of them, sitting next to me and pointing to my bowl, whispered gleefully into my ear, "Rats! Rats! You're eating rats!" No doubt he wished to stimulate my appetite.

I tried to ignore him. I was determined to fit in, to be accepted, to learn the ways of the "Real People" (which is what the name *Yup'ik* means). I thought to myself, *You're eating this too!* Besides, I really don't know what they stuff into hot dogs, either.

I had consumed most of the meat from my muskrat and finished my broth. The cook approached me. *"Taquten-qaa?"* (Are you finished?)

I thought I was, so I said *"Ii-i."* (Yes.)

She started to take away my bowl, but the expression on her face was not pleasant. Usually, when I answered appropriately or correctly she smiled, nodded, expressed approval. Now her face was blank. Something was amiss.

I changed my mind. *"Taqsaitua,"* I said. (I'm not done yet.)

She returned my bowl and walked away.

Now the problem was that I did not know why I was not done. But everyone else at the table was still very busy.

They were doing something common to all Alaska Native cultures, for which there is no English word. The Yup'ik word is *pukuq*, which means "to assiduously and carefully remove the meat from the bones of an animal so that none of it will be wasted, as a sign of gratitude and respect for the animal that allowed itself to be killed in order to feed you."

The universal belief among traditional people, certainly in Alaska and probably among hunting/gathering peoples throughout the world, is that a hunter catches only the animals who allow themselves to be caught. The animals are wiser and more sensitive than humans give them credit for. In fact, they are far more suited for survival in the Arctic than humans are.

Both the Yup'ik and the Tlingit nations tell a story about the arrival of the first people, who floated ashore in a device now described as a big clam shell. As they emerged, Raven, the leader of the animals, met them on the beach.

"What kind of thing are you?" Raven demanded. "I've never seen anything like you before!"

Circling around them, Raven shook his head disapprovingly. "Look at you! You have no feathers or wings! Obviously, you cannot fly.

"And look at your short, stubby legs! Clearly you cannot run very fast either.

"And your teeth! So small! What will you eat with those tiny fangs?

"And claws! Those pathetic fingers can't catch anything.

"Worst of all, you have hardly any fur! We have this

season called winter here. It is cold, below freezing more than half the year. There is simply no feasible way for you to survive the first winter here. You will die. Hypothermia will wipe you out during the first blizzard. You have no future in this country. Go back where you came from!"

The strange new arrivals refused.

"What am I going to do with you?" Raven demanded. He decided to call a convocation of all the arctic animals. He introduced the reason for the gathering by gesturing at the humans. "Look what I found on the beach this morning!" Raven shouted incredulously.

The other animals examined the People and quickly arrived at the same conclusions: they can't run, can't fly, can't grab or claw anything, can't eat very much, and, worst of all, they will soon freeze.

"Exactly!" Raven exclaimed. "I don't know what to do with them! I'm open to your suggestions. Anyone have any ideas?"

The others conferred most of the day and returned to Raven with a proposal. "What if we give these pathetic new creatures our fur and feathers for clothing, for cover? And what if we give them our bodies for food, as meat? Couldn't they survive then?"

Raven considered this. "You know, that just might work! They might survive if the rest of you are willing to die to clothe and feed them. But why would you do that? What do you want in exchange?"

And the animals replied, "We will give them our skins, our fur, and our feathers to use as cover, for clothing, and we will give them our flesh as meat, for food, in exchange for gratitude and respect."

And this is the agreement, the covenant, the First People made with the animals. Of course, I had never heard this story and knew nothing of this arrangement, but the muskrat meal showed me its primary ramification: When eating any meat, waste *nothing*!

So I did my best to imitate the behavior of my host and all the dinner guests. I separated every tiny bone from the others and, with some effort, gnawed and sucked and inhaled and slurped the meat from every muskrat bone until there was nothing left but a polished skeleton. My hostess and mentor returned and asked once more, "*Nutaan-qaa Taquten?*" (You're done now, aren't you?)

I replied with some hesitation, "*Ii-i.*"

She smiled and nodded. "*Ii-i!*"

But my lesson was not yet complete. One of the hunters came forward with a bucket and dumped the bones from all the empty bowls into it, took that bucket to his boat, and returned to the lake from which those muskrats had been harvested. He put the bones back into the water, returning, recycling them, and saying, "*Cali taikina!*" (Come back!)

If you have behaved humbly and respectfully toward a species, that species will continue to offer itself to you. If you have treated them badly, abusing, wasting, disrespecting the gift they offered, you should not expect any more of those resources. Those animals will withhold themselves from you, your family, perhaps even your village. We must all work together to relate to Nature with proper conduct, observing the established procedures and protocols in order to preserve the proper balance, the appropriate attitudes and behaviors.

Once, knowing how new and unfamiliar with the culture I was, one of my students played a hilarious joke on me.

I had developed the custom of sharing lunch with him every day that summer, and I entered his one-room cabin a little after noon. He was seated at the table, already eating.

Yup'ik people prefer silence. There is no need to speak if the situation is already obvious. In this case, since he was already having lunch, it was obvious that I should join him. We didn't need to discuss this. He did not need to serve me. The house was small. I knew where the bowls were and the drawer where the spoons were stored. The ladle was in the stewpot. It was a Yup'ik meal—boiled.

I dished myself a bowl of stew and sat down opposite him. He smiled and watched. I did not recognize the meat. It had been cut into wedges. The dark, almost black meat had a white layer of gristle and then skin with fur on it. I had to learn now to eat this food in the appropriate, respectful way, so I watched Phillip. He reached into his bowl, picked up a sliver of the meat, bit the dark part off, and set the fat and skin aside. *Okay! I can do this.*

I followed his example, lifted a chunk of meat from my bowl, bit off the dark part, and set aside the white, fatty, tough gristle with the skin and furry exterior attached.

Calmly and seriously, he asked, "Do you know what you are eating?"

"No," I replied. But I decided not to continue the conversation.

He waited for me to put another wedge of meat into my mouth and watched me chew. With an almost mournful expression, he continued, "One of our dogs died."

I was more than startled. There are dozens of sled dogs in every village, but they are fed only the leftovers, the garbage, whatever the people don't want or can't eat. *If you are what you eat, do I really want to eat dog?*

On the other hand, some cultures think of dog as a delicacy. Will he be offended if I spit this out?

What about the rule of respect? Does it apply to domesticated animals? Dogs can't give themselves the way wild animals do.

So if I consume this, will that be a sign of respect? If I don't, will it be an offense?

Back and forth I invisibly argued with myself until, at last, after five or more minutes of chewing and chewing and chewing, I finally swallowed that mouthful. And Phillip burst out laughing. "One of our dogs died—but this is walrus!"

This was not my last culinary test. Back in Sitka the previous semester, I had taken three Yup'ik students to a Mexican restaurant. It was obvious they were not accustomed to spicy food of any kind. The thick tomato sauces and peppers were alien to their tastes, and I commented on this as we left the café.

"I see you guys don't really like hot, spicy food."

"Yeah, that's true. Our traditional food does not have much flavoring. Nothing spicy. But don't worry. We have food we don't ever show white people."

I couldn't resist. "Like what?"

They looked at each other, a bit hesitant to discuss this topic. Then one of them volunteered, "We have something called *tepeq*. That name means 'stink.' We usually refer to them in English as stink heads."

"What are they? How are they prepared?"

"Well, they are not actually cooked, unless you consider fermenting in the ground to be a form of cooking."

"They're the heads of king salmon, wrapped usually in leaves or grass and buried in the ground for a few weeks. Then they are exhumed, washed off, and eaten. It's my favorite traditional food!"

I had no idea if I would or could eat such a dish, but I boldly offered to try it when the opportunity arose.

"No, you won't!" they insisted. "You'll take one whiff and walk away!"

EVERYDAY WONDERS

My opportunity arose on July 12, 1972, the Old Calendar feast of Ss. Peter and Paul, at about six PM. The local deanery clergy traditionally gathered at Kwethluk to celebrate the feast. Immediately after Liturgy, the priests and I were invited to Reader Paul's house. In honor of his name day, his family sponsored an all-day open house with food for anyone who would drop by. The priests were served a full breakfast with every conceivable appropriate food: eggs, bacon, ham, pancakes, fruit, homemade bread, butter, jam, hash, potatoes, juice, coffee, and tea. I ate my fill at the first sitting.

But as we gave thanks and adjourned, another man came forward from the shadows and took my arm.

"Where is he taking me?" I asked the others.

"To his house! They are waiting for you!"

"Waiting? Why?"

"They want you to share the feast with their son, Peter!"

Every family who had a father, brother, son, or uncle named either Peter or Paul had a feast that day, an open-house banquet that lasted all day. And in June, in Alaska, all day means about twenty-two hours! I think that day I was invited or shanghaied to a dozen different homes for breakfast, lunch, and/or dinner. Later in the day, the menu changed to wild meats of various sorts (seal, porcupine, beaver, moose, and even ham and turkey), salads, jello, and many kinds of *akutaq*—"Eskimo ice cream" made from mashed potatoes, shortening, oil, berries of every variety, and sometimes white fish.

By evening, I came waddling home. I had never eaten so much in one day in my life. I opened the door, and the fragrance of tepeq welcomed me into the house. I knew what it was immediately. I had never smelled anything like it before!

Sitting around a metal dish pan filled with fermented king salmon heads were five or six young Yup'ik guys, clearly relishing and enjoying the first stink heads of the summer season. One, who had been at the Mexican restaurant months before in Sitka, looked up at me with a smile. "Want to try some?"

It was he who had prophesied that I would "take one whiff" and refuse. I really had no physical room in my abdomen for any more food, but I knew that if I turned down the invitation now, I would probably never have the chance again. I would have reconfirmed their stereotype of kass'aaqs—that they never eat real Eskimo food.

So, with some hesitation, I sat on the floor and joined the tepeq banquet. It was slippery and smelly, but not at all bad-tasting. I had two heads. My friends became alarmed that such a rich, oily dessert might cause me some abdominal pain later, and one of them spent the night in an adjoining bed to monitor me. I had no problem. I did not realize it at the time, but I was about to become a cultural hero!

Villages on the Kuskokwim are fairly large and separated by only a few miles. The chain of villages runs along the entire length of the river, over eight hundred miles, but there are also villages along the various tributaries, including some off on the tundra between the Yukon and Kuskokwim Rivers. That August, for the first time, the regional church conference was being convened there, in the tundra village of Kasigluk, which lies at a distance of almost 80 miles by boat from Kwethluk. In 1972, there were no telephones in those villages. Communication was by word of mouth or by citizens' band (CB) radio. The "Tundra Drums" feature on the new public radio station, KYUK, would broadcast personal messages in English and Yup'ik twice a day, but this was not yet a common way of sending messages within the region.

I traveled through the maze of waterways, the rivers, sloughs, and lakes that connect those tundra villages to the main river, to attend a conference. This was the first time I had been to an Orthodox conference in Alaska, and I was eager to hear the singing—Orthodox services sung enthusiastically by hundreds of people who knew the texts by heart in their own language.

The tundra towns are wide-open, flat, waterlogged communities. In the soggy summer months, walking is practical only with the aid of the boardwalks that stretch across each village, allowing foot traffic between the school, the church, the store, and most homes. Walking around the village requires one to meet other pedestrians and greet them.

As I was walking toward Holy Trinity Orthodox Church in Kasigluk, I encountered a middle-aged man who not only greeted me but grabbed and shook my right hand vigorously.

Usually, upon being introduced, two Yup'iks will shake hands firmly but just once, performing a single downward pump. But this man shook my hand again and again, exclaiming, "Is it true what we hear? Is it true what they say about you?"

I had no idea how any rumor or report about me could have traveled this far from Kwethluk, nor what story he might have heard.

"We heard that you eat tepeq!"

Rivers, sloughs, lakes, streams, floods, and waterways could not prevent the amazing news from traveling nearly a hundred miles through the Y-K Delta. This guy eats stink heads!

I returned to St. Vladimir's to finish my final year of theological studies and, upon graduation, decided to let my friend in Kwethluk know when to expect me. I called KYUK in Bethel and asked if I could send a message to Xenia in Kwethluk using "Tundra Drums."

That week, for several days the same message was broadcast throughout the Delta: "To Xenia Angellan in Kwethluk from Michael in New York: I will arrive in Bethel at eleven AM on Saturday. Save some tepeq for me!"

I am told the entire region was roaring with laughter every time they heard that message broadcast across the watery paradise of the Yup'ik Nation.

✠ FOUR ✠

World War II and the ATG

FEW PEOPLE OUTSIDE ALASKA, or inside it for that matter, know that two islands in the Aleutian Archipelago were occupied by Japanese forces during the Second World War. Still fewer people, even among those interested in the history of that horrible and amazing era, recall that the entire Unangan Nation was interned in decrepit and unsanitary camps for most of the war years. Many died needlessly from malnutrition and disease due to neglect and indifference on the part of the very government that had removed them from their homes "for their own protection."

In World War II, Kodiak's uncooperative weather saved it from suffering a Japanese bombing raid. Its airport call letters remain ADQ, the abbreviation for Alaska Defense Headquarters. Large concrete bunkers still punctuate the otherwise pristine forest at Fort Abercrombie State Park on the northern edge of the city, and similar concrete fortifications guard the entry to Sitka. Realistically, though, there was never a significant threat from Japan's military forces. The occupation of Attu and Kiska was meant as a diversionary tactic, intended to draw off American naval forces before the showdown battle at Midway. Once the US scored its amazing victory there, the Japanese had no further hopes or plans to invade Alaska. The tide of battle had turned.

Nevertheless, the Unangan people were required to leave their homes and abandon their churches and community buildings to US military control. Citizens of little or no Alaska Native ancestry were allowed to remain in the Aleutian Islands. If there was a threat to the safety of civilians, it does seem odd that the evacuation order did not apply to everyone.

Aleut is a Russian word. Why Alaska Native people adopted it as their self-identity is a complex story. There may have been Siberian frontiersmen venturing into Alaskan waters as early as 1648.

Siberia itself had been penetrated, explored, mapped, and settled by frontiersmen over the last three centuries. A bachelor hunter and trapper would move beyond the borders of the empire in search of more plentiful game and better fishing, build a homestead, and set his trap lines. If he married at all, it would be with a local Siberian Native woman, and he would enjoy good trade and social relations with the local tribe. His children, of mixed parentage, would usually know both Russian and their mother's native tongue. They would move deeper into the wilderness, building their own outpost, marrying a local Siberian bride, and fathering another generation of mixed Slavic and indigenous children.

These are the kind of adventurous traders and trappers who came to Alaska. When history books refer to the "Russians" who ventured across the Bering Straits, we should be careful not to envision them as ethnically or racially Caucasian. They were required to apply for business licenses in Irkutsk, and a cursory examination of these applications indicates that about a third of them were Native people from Kamchatka, with another third being of mixed Slavic-Siberian backgrounds. The "Russians" who came to Alaska were therefore, more accurately, mostly Native people themselves.

Only naval officers, however, were given the privilege of naming the newly mapped islands. They usually chose the saint whose feast was being celebrated on the day they first sighted land. The islands in the Bering Sea reflect this pattern: St. Lawrence, St. Matthew, St. George, and St. Paul. The Orthodox churches on these islands have spring or summer feast days.

And so does St. Valentina, also known as Alevtina, or Aleutina.

In the mid-twentieth century, Unangan people, Alutiiq people, and even some Yup'ik people referred to themselves as "Aleut" when asked their tribe by an English speaker. These were, in pre-contact times, warring tribes, enemies. They robbed, raped, killed, and enslaved each other for centuries before the Siberian traders arrived. But they assumed a common Aleut identity in the past two hundred years. Where did this come from?

The simplest explanation has been to blame the confusion on the Russians. They did not recognize the difference between the tribes and simply mislabeled all those who lived on islands as Aleut, since they had named the entire archipelago for St. Alevtina. But this proves to be untrue. Gregory Shelikov, plotting to establish a permanent base on Kodiak Island, landed first at Unalaska to ransom a Kodiak prisoner of war, Kashpak, whom he brought back with him to Kodiak as an interpreter. The Russians knew the two tribes were incompatible and spoke mutually unintelligible languages before they arrived at Three Saints Bay in 1784.

Aleut is not a language. Aleuts speak Unangan, Alutiiq (Sugpiaq), and even Yup'ik. But for two centuries they also spoke Russian. They intermarried with Siberian Native frontiersmen and raised bilingual children, just as the Siberians had intermarried with Slavic pioneers during their exploration and settlement of Siberia. The pattern repeated in Alaska. Shelikov used harsh military methods to subdue the Kodiak Alutiiqs, and within a decade, his crew had married dozens of them. When the first Orthodox missionaries visited the

Aleutian Chain, they found hardly anyone to baptize—the frontiersmen had baptized their own wives and children and served as godfathers for each other's offspring. The priest was busy, instead, conducting weddings.

This intermarriage, as in Siberia, created a new and vibrant culture. When Father Gideon visited Kodiak, and later when St. Innocent Veniaminov arrived at Unalaska, they devised writing systems to record both Alutiiq and Unangan, so the next generation became literate in their local indigenous language and in Russian as well. When the US took control of Alaska in 1867, English was added to the curriculum of their schools. It was possible in 1970—one hundred years after the transfer to American rule—to meet Alaska Native elders who could read, write, and speak three languages in three alphabets. The mixed-race founder of what is today the Alaska State Historical Library and the Alaska State Museum, Father Andrew Kashevarov, spoke, read, and wrote Russian, Alutiiq, Tlingit, and English.

Listed as "Creole" in the Russian census, this population continued to grow while the Native population remained stagnant or declined. The false impression might be that the tribal peoples were dying off. In fact, they were just marrying each other. Creole teachers taught in bilingual schools. Creole priests preached and evangelized neighboring tribes. Creole sea captains delivered cargo and transported passengers to American, Asian, and European harbors. Creole graduates of the Russian Naval Academy mapped the Arctic coast and sailed around the world. In 1868, American statistics indicated that Sitka, the colonial capital, was over sixty percent Creole or Native, and Kodiak, the larger settlement, was ninety percent.

When a community identifies itself as Aleut, whether Unangan or Alutiiq, it is laying claim to this history. A culture is a story, not a language. The Swiss speak French, German, Italian, and Romanche, but their common history has created for them a Swiss identity, even though there is no language called "Swiss." This is also true for the Aleuts. Their story demonstrates that when an oppressed and enslaved people are given access to education, they can regain control of their lives and create a new hybrid culture, creatively combining their ancestral wisdom with new technology, and assume leadership roles in the new society they are themselves creating. It is an amazing and inspiring story.

Following the transfer of Alaska to American rule in 1867, this culture was maligned, attacked, and suppressed. American authorities were suspicious of a people who could read and write in languages the teachers and government officials did not understand. They were opposed to their continued use of their ancestral as well as their adopted languages, and they wrote forcefully of the need to eradicate this culture. World War II provided them with an opportunity to rid themselves of the Aleut people.

The internment camps to which the Aleuts were removed "for their own protection" were squalid and uninhabitable. Deprived of medicine and nutritious food, pregnant women lost their babies and often their lives in the camps. Elders who could not adjust to the cold dampness of Southeast Alaska's rainforests also succumbed under these conditions. Without any job opportunities, men sat idle for months at a time. Summoned to return to their island homes to harvest fur seals, the Pribilof men from St. Paul and St. George were promised bonus pay for working in what was still considered a war zone. But such promises were never kept. The federal government profited from the sale of the fur seal pelts, earning nearly one million 1944 dollars, but the laborers received less than minimum wage.

When they were finally repatriated to their villages, the Aleuts found that their homes and churches had been ransacked and vandalized by soldiers, not from Japan but from the US. Some of the Natives were never permitted to return to their homes but had to build new lives and new homes elsewhere. For the next forty years, the Aleutian landscape was strewn with military debris, rusting tanks and jeeps, decaying bunkhouses, and Quonset huts. Dutch Harbor in 1975 looked like Berlin in 1945—hundreds of rotting, roofless, window-shattered buildings labeled "US Government Property: No Salvaging." It took the Aleuts a decade of lawsuits and finally an act of Congress to win an apology for their mistreatment—and to be paid a nominal reparation award that was one-fourth as much as was issued to Japanese-Americans for their horrible wartime treatment.

This was not a single episode, an event of limited duration, like a traffic accident. This situation lasted four years. This was a policy, an attempt to disrupt and destroy a culture and a tribe. Today, if we examine Alaska's history textbooks, the contributions and accomplishments of the Aleut people—and in fact the very existence of their culture—are completely ignored, as are the story of their internment and the suppression of their languages and history. It is as if they never existed at all and these injustices were never perpetrated on them.

The Yup'ik people escaped all this trouble and trauma. Left to themselves on their windswept tundra straddling the Nushagak, Kuskokwim, and Yukon Rivers and the shores of Lake Iliamna, the Yup'ik and Inupiaq men were instead organized to defend their homeland from Japanese invasion in a military unit named the Alaska Territorial Guard (ATG). They were inducted with the usual physical exams and basic training routine, issued rifles and white uniforms, and organized into village platoons. They felt honored to be called upon to defend their country and proud to be of service to Uncle Sam.

I knew little of the Alaska Territorial Guard until I proposed to my wife. Knowing that my father-in-law's grasp of English was limited, I decided to introduce the topic of marriage, and hopefully gain his approval for it, through the not-so-subtle method of placing the four wedding candles I had already purchased on the kitchen table. I sat patiently waiting for Adam to arrive.

When he came in, he walked by me, paused, looked at the table, and said out loud in English, "Hmm. Wedding candles!"

But he passed by and went into the adjoining room for a few minutes. When he returned, he sat down next to me and said, "During the Big War, I was in the ATG."

Yes, I knew this already, but I was not particularly interested in hearing more about the guard just then. I had more important questions to resolve.

He began to talk about "Muktuck" Marston, the colonel whose idea it had been to create the ATG.

I picked up two of the candles, and Adam paused. "Yes, I see. Wedding candles. Wait!"

And he continued his story about enlisting in the Territorial Guard and what their daily routine had been.

I tried to introduce the wedding into the conversation, but Adam continued rambling about where they had to go to sign up and how they all got dogtags.

Yes, I thought, *that's the normal routine, but what about me marrying your daughter?*

And then he came to the point. He was issued his identification tags, and the officer who presented them asked, "Are you really Yup'ik?

No one had ever doubted that Adam Andrew was one hundred percent Yup'ik. He spoke the language fluently and was a master storyteller and an excellent provider for his family. Of course he was Yup'ik. But he had never known his father.

"Well," the officer continued, "you have a blood type that is not normally found among Yup'ik people."

Then Adam got up to leave.

I picked up the wedding candles once more.

"Yes! Wedding candles! I'm not the boss. Ask her mother!" And he walked out the door.

But I had my answer. If he was himself a Creole, if there was some Siberian or Russian ancestor in his background, if Adam himself was not one hundred percent Yup'ik, how could he object to his daughter marrying a kass'aaq? As Dr. Lydia Black used to say, "Pure breeds exist only in dog shows."

But if it had not been for World War II and the ATG, would we ever have found out?

✠ FIVE ✠

Lost and Found

FATHER VASILY EPCHOOK was the son of Archpriest Nicolai Epchook and the father of the priest Stephen Epchook. Fluent in Yup'ik and English, Father Vasily also served capably in Church Slavonic, ministering in Egegik, New Stuyahok, Gillingham, and Lower Kalskag. He remembers as a child being held and taught by Bishop Amphilokhy Vakulsky, the vicar bishop of Alaska in the early twentieth century. Most of his education, however, came from his kindly father, who, as pastor of St. Nicholas Church in Kwethluk, went door to door each day to personally invoke God's blessings on every household in the community, Orthodox or not.

Father Vasily was a man of many talents. He created works of art for the churches he served and helped design several of the buildings. One of his most unusual creations was a pectoral cross, made for a priest to wear, carved from the antler of a moose. It was this moose-antler cross that inspired others later to carve crosses in walrus ivory, but the antler allowed for greater detail. The design was simple and clear. The cross measured about four inches tall and three inches wide, bearing a depiction in outline form of the outstretched body of Jesus Christ, the sign written by Pontius Pilate over His head, and the skull of Golgotha below His feet.

This moose-antler cross was given to me on the day I was ordained, the Feast of the Prophet Elias on the Old Calendar, August 2. The cross itself was very light, almost weightless. At one point I had small metal tabs glued onto the back of it to hold it down, since the chain on which it hung was heavier than the cross itself, and the cross kept sliding up my chest as the chain pulled down my back.

I wore this cross from the day of my ordination for many years. Father Vasily also gave me a silver cross, the one he had been given at his ordination. When his son Stephen was ordained, I passed the silver cross on to him, but I kept the unique moose-antler cross for myself as Father Vasily's personal gift to me, his godson.

My wife and I were married in April, during the season Alaskans call "breakup." The river was thawing, and the landing strip was becoming incredibly muddy. The paths through the village were extremely slippery. The flowers and tuxedos had arrived in Bethel, seventeen miles downriver, but fetching them proved difficult. The plane that brought the last wedding guests slid sideways down the runway and nearly crashed.

Since most of the village schoolchildren knew both me and my bride, the teachers dismissed classes early so the entire student body could attend. They came equipped with bags of raw rice, which they jubilantly tossed around us as we left the church, chasing us along the slippery paths.

There are no reception halls or community gathering facilities in the village, so couples rush home and welcome friends and relatives in an all-day open house, where most of the village eventually dines, one sitting after the next, until all have enjoyed the banquet. So many people jammed themselves into my in-laws' frame house that the temperature rose until the icing on our wedding cake melted, oozing down its four- or five-layered sides like a magnificent white waterfall.

The final obstacle to our escape downriver to Bethel, the airport, and our wedding night at the Captain Cook Hotel was finding a place along the riverbank solid enough to support us, the snow machine, and the sled. Xenia spent the ride down the frozen river seated on the snow machine, while I was dragged behind in the sled. The treads of the snow machine threw back enough slush to cover me long before we reached the airport.

In Anchorage, we were welcomed with a second wedding reception on the front lawn of St. Innocent Cathedral, blessed by the bishop, and treated to a second wedding cake, whose frosting held tight. Father Nicholas Molodyko-Harris was responsible for getting us to our connecting flight later that week, but his school bus route ran late that morning. We had no alternative but to jump onto it and rush to the airport to catch our flight. In Sitka we took the shore boat to get into the town, and in New York we traveled by train and bus. I think on our honeymoon we used every known means of transport except a rickshaw! At my parents' home in Pennsylvania, we were treated to a third reception and a third magnificent cake, which also retained its icing. Two out of three isn't bad!

In all Orthodox weddings, the bridal couple are attended by another Orthodox man and woman, sometimes known as the best man and maid (or matron) of honor, sometimes as the sponsors. In our corner of Orthodoxy, couples being married normally choose an older married couple they know, love, and respect to fill this role, and they become the godparents of the couple as a couple. This establishes a trusting relationship between the younger and older couples, binding them together in mutual love and support. The idea is that the younger couple then have a more experienced husband and wife to whom they can turn in case they have any problems, difficulties, or temptations in their marriage.

Originally my fiancée and I had chosen my Yup'ik "parents," Annabelle and William Olick, to be our godparents, but in the months before our wedding, William died. Xenia sewed beautiful light blue *kaspeqs*[*] for both Annabelle and Matushka Euphemia Epchook to wear to our wedding ceremony, but it was the Epchooks who served as godparents on our actual wedding day, April 26, 1974. It was because of this special relationship we already enjoyed that Father Vasily carved me the world's only moose-antler cross as a gift for my ordination three months later.

Eventually, Xenia fashioned a beautiful beaded chain for this cross, using old Russian trade beads and bone to highlight the light-brown hues of the antler. But after it had seen two decades of use, a young toddler grabbed the beaded chain and pulled it hard enough to break the threads. The beads and the cross itself fell to the floor of my sister-in-law Minnie's house.

Since I could not wear it any longer, Minnie put the cross on the shelf in the icon corner, commenting that I should not forget to take it home when we returned from Kwethluk to Juneau. But a week later, when we were departing, I could not find the cross anywhere.

"Don't worry," Minnie assured me. "It'll turn up. I'll clean the house thoroughly next week, and I'm sure I'll find it."

But she didn't.

Years passed. Every time I returned to Kwethluk I inquired about the cross, but no one had found it.

More than a decade later, my brother-in-law, Max, came to visit our house in Anchorage.

---

[*] An embellished blouse with a hood and patch pocket.

"Something amazing happened a few years ago," he said.

"Really? What was that?"

"I was out hunting some distance from the village, out in the wilderness, and I spotted something smooth on the ground. It was brown and blended into the ground, almost camouflaged."

"What was it?"

"When I picked it up and turned it over, it turned out to be a cross. I took it home and put in my icon corner. After a few years I decided it was too nice a cross not to be used, so I put it on a cord and started wearing it." And Max pulled out from under his shirt the mysteriously missing moose-antler cross!

Moose and deer shed their antlers every year, and these dissolve into the ground during the winter. This fragment of an antler would normally have been absorbed into the earth in a few weeks. Laying aside the question of how the cross left my sister-in-law's house and traveled out onto the tundra, it is amazing that it should have been found so soon, let alone by a relative of mine who could then, knowing nothing of its origins, travel hundreds of miles to unwittingly bring it back to me.

Incredible coincidences. But then, I no longer believe in coincidence.

✠SIX✠

Receiving My ThD

I NEVER CONSCIOUSLY DECIDED to pursue a doctoral degree. It just happened.

After being invited to join the faculty of Alaska Pacific University in Anchorage, I was engaged by the College of Rural and Human Development, an odd amalgam of the Departments of Rural Development and Education, to conduct training for the XCOP, their incredibly thorough summer Cross-Cultural Orientation Program. Teachers who were seeking positions in Alaska enrolled in this six-week course and were prepared, much like Peace Corps volunteers, for their entrance into another culture, not knowing which it would be. Alaska has twenty indigenous languages and hundreds of federally recognized tribes, and venturing into any one of them requires the same kind of training as going to work overseas.

EVERYDAY WONDERS

As the situation at APU became less and less comfortable and budget cuts made continuing on the faculty there less appealing, the dean in Fairbanks was becoming increasingly interested in hiring me there. As one opportunity seemed to be evaporating, another was coming to a boil. I went to Fairbanks as the temporary replacement for a brilliant colleague and friend and wound up staying on in a program with another X-rated name: X-CED. This acronym stood for the Cross-Cultural Education Development program. In this program, teachers' assistants were given the opportunity to climb up the career ladder by taking the courses they would need to become certified staff and assume the position of a full-fledged classroom teacher, with its attendant salary and benefits.

During every year of its operation, X-CED graduated more Alaska Natives than all the other programs and colleges combined. It did so by bringing the course materials and instructors into the villages rather than requiring students to move to the campus. X-CED's students were overwhelmingly adult female community leaders, wives, mothers, and grandmothers, for whom leaving their village to attend college full-time was completely impractical and even unthinkable. They would have to leave the very job that made them interested in attaining a bachelor's degree in order to earn one. X-CED enabled them to earn that degree without leaving their village or family.

Receiving My ThD

My MDiv was initially accepted as a terminal degree at UAF because there was no school in North America that could award a doctoral degree in my field, Orthodox theology. However, some hints were dropped suggesting that without a doctorate I might not be offered tenure. It was Archbishop Anastasios Yannoulatos, at that time working in Kenya, who suggested that I pursue a degree at the University of Athens, Greece. He had met me at several international missions conferences and was interested in promoting my academic career, though it was never the main focus of my life.

"Send me what you have written, and I can have a committee at our theological school examine it. If they accept you, you can get your doctoral degree from us in Athens," he said.

I did. But then the archbishop was transferred to Albania, and we lost touch. The remaining members of the committee did not know me personally and began making additional and eventually impossible demands. Could I prepare a translation of my dissertation in Greek? I was already working with nineteenth-century Russian manuscripts and archival sources that often included Yup'ik and Aleut authors. Adding Greek to the list of necessary languages seemed to be an unassailable wall. I did contact and even pay some Greek graduate students at Oxford to begin translating some of my writings, but I never got a single page from them.

Discouraged, I was ready to give up on any possibility of

earning a doctoral degree, when I was invited to a Syndesmos (World Orthodox Youth Federation) conference in Presov, CSSR. The Czechoslovak Socialist Republic had been forcibly kept within the communist bloc by a 1968 invasion led by armed forces from the Soviet Union. I was apprehensive about entering an occupied country.

We went by night train to Presov and were warmly welcomed at the seminary campus. On a tour of the facility, I noticed several shelves of doctoral dissertations, bound and neatly displayed in the library.

"You have a doctoral program here?" I inquired timidly.

"Yes, of course. Why do you ask?"

I told them my situation.

"Send what you have written to us, and we will take a look at it."

I did. They did. Three years later, I was invited to defend my dissertation and sit for oral comprehensive examinations in church history and patristics.

My doctoral defense required many extra hours of interrogation, mostly because my fluency in spoken Russian was very limited. I had worked with archives and documents for years, but I hadn't had to speak Russian since my senior year at Georgetown, where I was able to sit for one semester of intensive Russian with Mr. Lager. The class was quite intimidating. We had to rise when called upon (in front of a class of several hundred peers) and recite the appropriate answer perfectly, without stumbling or a trace of accent—or be humiliated.

But my doctoral committee was civil, courteous, and very professional. Father Pavel began by flattering me, saying that they had all learned so much about Alaska and the story of Orthodox Christianity there, so we should begin the process as an informal conversation between colleagues. Father Stefan protested immediately, insisting that we were engaged in a rigorous academic examination. And so, for the next three hours, they played the roles of good cop/bad cop, the one asking questions that required considerable reflection and detail, the other probing with questions that could be answered in a sentence or two. In the end, they unanimously agreed to award me the Doctor of Theology degree.

If I had presented my dissertation, "The Development of the Aleut Identity," to a committee of Alaskan scholars, the discussion might have become a lot more heated and uncomfortable, with the Anglo professors denying the factual basis of my entire dissertation. An earlier essay I had written broaching the subject, entitled "Three Saints Bay," was rejected as fiction. Only when I appealed to the Department of the Interior, which had funded the research, and insisted that all my footnotes and references be re-examined by a competent archivist at the Library of Congress was my paper accepted and the honorarium paid.

My dissertation dealt with how literacy in their own language and alphabet created the impetus and means by which Alaska Native people rose to the level of an indigenous intelligentsia, translating and writing their own books and opening their own schools. This led, I discovered, to the next generation building their own churches, operating their own schools, trading posts, and even hospitals, sailing their own ships, and conducting their own commerce.

This is a unique history that has hardly been explored and is, in fact, readily denied by scholars in the field. There is a prejudice, a bias that prevents experts from acknowledging that tribal peoples can accomplish this sort of successful adaptation in two or three generations. The territorial and federal governments have been struggling with this problem for over a century, without success. No one wants to admit that the Russian colonial administration succeeded in thirty years in doing what the US had not managed in a hundred and fifty.

The Russians only brought to Alaska the same attitudes and procedures by which they had been "civilized" in the days of Prince Vladimir, who adopted Orthodoxy for Kievan Rus' in 988. At that time the Russians inherited the work done by Saints Cyril and Methodius generations earlier, when they created a written Slavonic language for the Moravian people and translated the biblical and liturgical texts into it from the Greek. The Russians gave the Unangan and Alutiiq, as well as some Yup'ik and Tlingit people, their own alphabet, then translated and published textbooks in those languages. Within a generation or two, the Natives were translating or even writing their own. It really doesn't take that long. But there are still those today—like the Bavarians who opposed Cyril and Methodius and drove them out of Moravia, claiming that only Greek and Latin were fit for expressing the Christian faith—who insist that education can be conducted only in their own "civilized" language.

What does it take to produce a Doctor of Theology? A lot of love and encouragement in childhood, some remarkable teachers and professors at all levels of education, followed by a lot of wise and generous colleagues, supportive friends, a loving wife with patient and forgiving children, a welcoming and hospitable review committee, a socialist government that doesn't know what tuition is or how much to charge, and finally, one of the earliest computers Apple ever produced. Add to this a desire to visit the ancestral homeland, and presto! You get a ThD—even if you never really needed it and won't refer to it, rely on it, or cite it ever again. But I can now sign my name with three letters after it: Very Rev. Michael J. Oleksa, ThD.

✠ SEVEN ✠

Roots Trips: 1988, 1999, 2014

I ALWAYS WANTED to find out where Baba, my grandmother, was born.

One of the most attractive aspects of the decision to continue my doctoral work at the Orthodox Theological Faculty in Presov, Slovakia, was that the location brought me to less than a hundred miles from the birthplaces of my paternal grandparents, John Oleksa and Anna Dorosz. They had immigrated to the US early in the twentieth century from villages on the north slope of the Carpathian Mountains, between the Polish city of Sanok and the Slovakian city of Presov. Defending my dissertation and receiving my Doctor of Theology degree there would give my family the first opportunity in nearly a century to revisit my ancestral homeland and, perhaps, make contact with some surviving relatives.

EVERYDAY WONDERS

In June of 1988, therefore, my parents, my Aunt Mary, my wife, and our four children piled into a bright-red rented Volkswagen nine-passenger van and drove from Munich to Vienna, to Budapest, and then north to Presov. We were welcomed royally to the quaint medieval city, and once the academic procedures were successfully completed, my father hosted a banquet to celebrate the achievement. Archbishop Nikolai, the members of my committee, and the nine members of the Oleksa family enjoyed a wonderful meal with much friendly chatter and laughter.

The next morning we departed eastward, toward the Soviet border. Twice over we were required to unload the van, unpack all our suitcases, and allow the officials to inspect everything in our possession. When they had finished, we had to repack, reload, and leave. Each inspection lasted over three hours, and since there is a one-hour time change between the countries, we wasted a total of seven daylight hours at that border.

By the time we arrived in Uzhgorod, in Transcarpatia, the sun was already setting, and our hotel reservations were prepaid. My hope of seeing some of the Ukrainian countryside as we crossed the Carpathians was vanquished by the impending darkness.

We arrived in L'viv long after sunset, and the streetlights went off at about ten PM. We asked directions for the Dniester Hotel (the name of one of the two rivers that join in the center of Ukraine and flow to the Black Sea), but there was none. However, there was a prominent Dnieper Hotel (named for the other major river). The travel agent had typed the name of the wrong river.

"Where have you been?" the desk clerk barked at me. "We have been waiting all day for you!"

"At *your* border!" I replied with some irritation, and she quietly gave us our room keys. But I had no idea why she was so upset. What did it matter to her what time we arrived at the hotel?

Having prepaid for everything essential for our visit through the Soviet Intourist agency, we were entitled to breakfast at the Dnieper Hotel restaurant, and our table awaited us at eight AM. After the meal we descended to the lobby, where another lady met us. Timidly, hesitantly, this little middle-aged Ukrainian lady tugged my sleeve and asked, "*Ty Otyets Mikhailo Oleksa?*" (Are you Father Michael Oleksa?)

"*Tak!*" (Yes!)

The woman began to cry. She was Katerina Kalanich, my father's cousin, the one member of the Dorosz family who wrote consistently to me and my Aunt Mary. The family reunion had begun. Katerina and Mikhailo Sedor and their daughter Halina then stepped forward to introduce themselves. Both Katherines were my father's first cousins, and as my aunt, parents, and family entered the lobby, there were hugs, kisses, and tears all around. The American and European branches of the family were being reconnected. This was why the hotel clerk had been so upset—she had seen our cousins sitting in the lobby for hours the previous day!

We left the VW van in L'viv and set off eastward by train to Ternopil, since Soviet travel rules forbade foreigners to bring their own vehicles any further into Ukraine. After a night at the Moskva (Moscow) Hotel, we boarded a minibus our relatives had rented and set out for their village homes, stopping to pray at the graves of relatives who were buried along the route.

This was not my grandmother's birthplace. Our family had lived for centuries in the Carpathian Mountains, but in 1945, an act of the Polish Parliament expelled them (and all non-Poles) from the newly defined borders of post-war Poland and sent them either to the newly annexed German region to the west or into the USSR to the east. Operation Vistula constituted Allied-sponsored relocation—what would now be termed "ethnic cleansing." Over 200,000 Rus (both Orthodox and Ukrainian Catholic) were exiled from their villages, their homes and churches were burned, and their cemeteries were desecrated, in scenes recalling the finale to *Fiddler on the Roof.*

Sitting around a huge table with dozens of cousins and their spouses and children crammed into the room, Aunt Mary passed an old photo over to Helena, my grandmother's youngest sister. The photo had been brought to America by my grandmother's youngest brother, Nicolas, and showed an older man with a full head of thick white hair and a huge mustache. Nicolas was dead, and none of us knew who this man was.

Aunt Helen recognized the man immediately. "This is my father!" she pronounced with joy. As she handed the photo to me, she added, "And today he is smiling."

Our visit to the village, Pidruda, was much too brief, but we had limited time on our Soviet visas and had to return to L'viv and then enter Poland. I yearned to return and have another chance to reconnect with these hospitable and warm-hearted distant relatives.

We returned to our nine-passenger van and drove west to Sanok, found our hotel, and rested. We discovered the marvelous Skanzen, the open-air museum of Carpathian folk life, complete with authentic houses, churches, and structures that had survived Operation Vistula, as well as a museum of folk icons rescued from the demolished or burned churches. We were looking at cabins and homes similar to the one in which my grandmother had been born a century earlier. We were getting close!

We knew that my grandmother's village, Khotsin, no longer existed. Aunt Helen and Cousin Hanya had told us the story of how the soldiers came to expel them from their homes. The peasants refused to leave. The army then came with rifles and began shooting the livestock—chickens, geese, and cows. The villagers then surrendered, agreeing to be loaded onto boxcars and shipped by train to western Ukraine, much as Holocaust victims had been shipped to their deaths under Nazi occupation just a few years before. The region they were headed for had been invaded and heavily bombed by the German army in 1942 and then fought over until 1944. Hardly any buildings were left standing, and the fields were filled with mines and bombs. But this was where they were shipped, hundreds of thousands of my father's people.

When the soldiers came to remove the Dorosz family, my grandmother's father, Stefan (the man in the photo), lay sick and dying. The officers said the family could stay until he died. Consequently, they witnessed the burning of the village and church and the destruction of the cemetery. The goal was to eliminate any vestige of their presence, to erase all memory that a village had ever existed on that site. On Old Calendar Theophany, January 19, Stefan Dorosz died, and the family had to bury him themselves in what had been the parish cemetery, near the ruins of the church, on the other side of the creek that flowed through the now-deserted village of Khotsin.

Finding even the ruined village would have been impossible, except that my grandmother's Aunt Anastasia had gone to America long before, then returned and married a Polish man. Her children had not been expelled in 1945, since they had assimilated into Polish society. Her daughter, Maria, met us in Sanok and guided us to where she thought Khotsin had once stood. We had a memorial service there, after we found a cross among the brush and weeds that had overgrown the site. A neighbor emerged from a nearby house and asked who we were, where were we from. Much to our amazement, the lady had a sister living not just in America but in Pennsylvania, and not just Pennsylvania but specifically Allentown. Aunt Mary knew her! What a small world!

We then began our search for John Oleksa's birthplace, Szczawno, a village that had survived Operation Vistula, and its church, the Church of the Dormition of the Virgin Mary. I could locate the village on a map that also indicated the approximate location of the old wooden chapel. We drove through the village once, twice, three times. There were no side streets—just one road that ran in one side and out the other—but we found no sign of the church. Maria said she thought there was one old man in this town who had refused to leave, barricaded himself in his house, and, despite the loss of water, heat, and electricity, stubbornly resisted all attempts to exile him. She believed that this man, Nikolai Matsko, might still be there. Finding his dilapidated old cottage, she and Aunt Mary (who, as the oldest of my grandmother's children, spoke the local language the most fluently) entered.

Returning excitedly to our van, they explained that Mr. Matsko did have the keys to the church, which was camouflaged and could not easily be seen from the road, but that he had lent the keys to someone else who was making some minor repairs. But if we drove down the road, crossed the railroad tracks, and turned right, we would spot the church on the hill. Delighted, we drove down the road and crossed the railroad tracks. But a cornfield greeted us. There was no path, no road, and no sign of a church or even a hill. Maybe we had misunderstood?

We returned to Mr. Matsko's house, and he offered to squeeze into our already crowded van and show us the way. When we reached the cornfield, he insisted we plow through.

"Into the corn?" I exclaimed. "Won't the owner object?"

"Never mind! "

Once we had flattened four or five rows of corn, we entered a meadow, beyond which was a forested hillside, on the top of which stood the church for which we had been so diligently searching. We climbed up, and Mr. Matsko began reminiscing.

"Oleksa . . . Oleksa? . . . Oleksa! Yes! Oleksa!" He remembered. "Yes, two brothers . . . they went to America when I was a boy. One of them got married first, here, at this church. Yes! After the ceremony they put me on the bride's lap. They said that it would be good luck, that she would have many sons!"

My grandfather John had come to America with his older brother Wasyl (Basil) and Wasyl's wife, Mary. Mary had to remain in Szczawno longer than expected. The outbreak of the First World War forced her to live there until the war ended in

1918, after which she was able to emigrate with her son John, by then a four- or five-year-old boy. Mary Oleksa did in fact have two more sons in America—apparently, Nikolai Matsko brought her the good fortune the villagers had predicted.

Without Mr. Matsko's help, we would never have found that camouflaged church. He even recalled the unmarked grave of my great-grandparents, Kondrat and Barbara Oleksa. I resolved to return someday and put up a cross to mark their burial site. I also wanted to go inside the church and pray there, even celebrate the Liturgy, if I could—someday.

In August 1999, I had the opportunity to visit Szczawno again. I knew how to find the church by then, so I parked the rental car and climbed the hill. I realized that Mr. Matsko had been quite elderly when we met him in 1988, so I walked around the church to the cemetery. His was the first grave I met. The stone cross on his grave included an embossed photo of him as a young man, sixty years before. The inscription startled me, however: it showed that he had died six weeks after our visit in 1988. If he had left this world a few weeks earlier, we never would have found the place nor known of the gravesite of my great-grandparents. More amazingly, I had arrived on the eleventh anniversary of his death. I immediately sang the entire memorial service at his grave. *Vechnaya Pamyat!* May his memory be eternal!

Four years later, I was in Joensuu, Finland, visiting the Orthodox seminary there, and asked the librarian if I could check my email. My father had been ill for months and was failing rapidly, so I needed to know how he was doing. The librarian got me online, and I read a message from my sister, "Call home." I had a pretty good idea what the news would be, but I had to speak to her. I asked the librarian (in Russian) if I could find a phone anywhere.

"Yes," he said. "There is a land-line attached to the fax machine in the dean's office, down the hall." And he gave me the keys.

I found the office, the fax, and the attached phone, called Pennsylvania, and learned that my father had died a few hours before. I promised to find a flight back to the United States as soon as a seat was available.

I returned the keys to the librarian.

"Is everything okay?" he asked politely.

"Well, no, my father just died."

"Oh! I'm sorry to hear that . . ."

"You're not from here, from Finland, are you?" I asked.

"No, actually, I'm from Poland."

"Really? I've been there several times."

"To Warsaw? Krakow?"

"No, in fact, Sanok."

"Sanok? Why would you go to Sanok?"

"My father's parents were both born in villages near Sanok."

"Really! Exactly which villages?"

"My grandmother's village, Khotsin, no longer exists. It was destroyed in 1945."

"Ah! Operation Vistula . . ."

"Yes . . . but my grandfather's village survived, and even the church still stands."

"Wow! Which village was that?"

"Not a very big place. It's the village of Szczawno."

"Szczawno! Szczawno! My father was the priest in Szczawno!"

"No! That's amazing! You know, it is really hard to find the church there."

"Yes! I know! You have to cross the railroad tracks and plow through that cornfield."

"We went there for the first time in 1988 and could not find it."

"Did you locate the church eventually?"

"Yes, with the help of an old gentlemen, Nikolai Matsko."

"Nikolai Matsko! My father's best friend!"

The librarian, whose name was Father Alexander, then told me that a younger priest, Father Julian Felenczak, served that village now. Father Julian, however, does not speak English or Russian. He studied at the seminary in France, married a Parisian woman, and speaks the local Rus language, Polish, and French. How good was my French? Well, I had three years in high school, so it would have to suffice. Father Alexander, a Polish librarian in Finland, provided me with the email address of the French-speaking pastor who serves my grandfather's village.

Through Father Julian, we erected memorial crosses at my great-grandparents' gravesite in Szczawno, and after several attempts at various seasons of the year, with the help of Father Julian and his parishioners, we were able to locate the actual Khotsin village site and plant a cross there in memory of my grandmother's parents. Then, much to my delight and surprise, during a visit in 2008, we discovered that the Polish National Forest Service had excavated the village of Khotsin, as if it were an ancient archeological site. They marked each house and fenced the cemetery, marking with a pile of stones the place where the church's altar had once stood. So in 2014 I returned to that spot to bless and dedicate a memorial cross on which are inscribed the names of Stefan and Ekaterina Dorosz. I sang the Paschal Troparion, *Khristos Voskrese*: "Christ is risen from the dead, trampling down death by death, and upon those in the tombs bestowing life!"

I felt that by placing a cross at the place where the altar once stood, I had brought to closure my roots exploration and honored my ancestors. I ensured, as best I could, that their burial sites would be known, and that even in this world their memory would not be lost.

Now it is our prayer that God will also remember them in eternity. *Vechnaya Pamyat!*

✠ EIGHT ✠

Suceava

I ALWAYS WANTED to go to Suceava, even though I didn't know how to pronounce it. At seminary I had seen the album cover of an LP of Romanian *colinde*, Christmas carols, on which was depicted a beautifully frescoed church, painted not on the interior but on the outside. Yes, the icons were on the exterior of the church and had withstood hundreds of years of wind, rain, snow, frost, and hail.

I had been invited to Europe for a conference but booked an earlier flight so I could travel to Romania before my meetings convened in Germany. I flew into Warsaw and happened across a quartet of seminarians from the Warsaw seminary planning to leave the next day by car for Bucharest. They had room for me, and I gladly joined their pilgrimage south.

We slept in and around the car in Debrecen, Hungary,

and arrived in Cluj Napoca, Romania, in the province of Transylvania, on a Sunday morning. The larger churches of the town were built when Transylvania was part of the Austro-Hungarian Empire and were therefore Roman Catholic. The Orthodox majority could hardly find a building in which to gather for their worship, and most of the Orthodox temples were small and obscure—but we found one. I had attended a Romanian parish in my senior year at St. Vlad's, so I was able to join the congregational singing. We finished the day by driving south to Bucharest, where I bade farewell to my Polish companions and caught a train north.

I got to Suceava, the capital of Bukovina, after dark and used my guidebook to decide where to spend the night. I decided on the Bukovina Hotel, since we were in that province, and instructed the cab driver to take me there. Upon arrival, I was convinced I had chosen wisely: the lobby was decorated with huge photos of five painted monasteries, all within a few hours' drive of the city.

At check-in, I asked the desk clerk about arranging a driver to take me to the monasteries whose images adorned the surrounding walls. She knew very little English but indicated that I could more economically take the city bus to each of them, visiting one each day for the next five days. I explained that I did not have five days to spend there and needed to find a way to make a single day's excursion, the next day or the day after at the latest. She gave the impression that she had never heard of such a ridiculous idea, but she promised to investigate further.

The next morning, she informed me that there was no one available to take me on this extraordinary trip, but she had engaged a car and driver for me for the following day, if I could pay two hundred dollars for the day. I thought this was probably the only opportunity I would ever have to see these amazing churches, so I agreed to the rather exorbitant price. When else would I ever come to Romania, to Bukovina, to the land of the painted monasteries?

I spent that day exploring the city, whose name, I learned, is pronounced Sue-CHA-vah. I discovered that a Big Mac by any other name is just as greasy, but at least I knew what I was getting. The highlight was the monastery of St. John the New Martyr, whose body had been rescued from the Turkish-occupied portion of the Balkans and enshrined in Suceava. When the Ottomans threatened to conquer the city, his coffin was taken to Poland briefly but then returned, and a beautiful and unique cathedral was built to welcome St. John home. This journey was very similar to the one my ancestors made, leaving their ancestral home near Storozhnets, just north of Suceava, for what is now Poland. They, however, never returned to their Bukovinian homeland, being exiled instead to Ukraine.

The next morning, the manager of the hotel, Mr. Dimitrie Maerean, welcomed me to the hotel vehicle. He indicated he did not speak English but had a tour guide and translator lined up for our day-long journey to the painted monasteries. We had driven about two kilometers from the Bukovina Hotel when he pulled off the road, parked the car, and left me sitting, waiting in the back seat. He was gone for a surprisingly long time, but he eventually returned with a young man about twenty years old.

With a big smile, the young man introduced himself, shook my hand, and said, "I am Ionut Maerean. I will be your tour guide today."

"Wonderful, thank you! You speak English very well. How did you learn it?

"From watching the Discovery Channel," he answered.

And off we went. A tremendous summer cloudburst interrupted our drive, but we soon arrived at the monastery of Humor. Surrounding the monastery on all sides were handmade woolen rugs. The local villagers not only raise sheep but shear the wool, spin and dye it, and weave traditional rugs in every size, color, and design. At that time, before Romania entered the European Union, these folk masterpieces were incredibly inexpensive. But I was not in the market for rugs on that day. Where was the church?

Inside the walls of the Humor monastery was a real jewel of a church, still partly covered with beautiful Byzantine iconography. The next stop, Voronet, was even more spectacular. Its eastern wall is covered with a huge fresco of the Last

Judgment. Depicted on a background of the color known as Voronet blue is an icon ten meters tall. Central and topmost is Christ on His Throne, before whom all peoples and nations appear, with the Twelve Apostles seated below Him assisting in the tribunal. On His right are the martyrs and saints from all ages, gazing lovingly at their Lord. On His left are those who rejected Him or refused to believe in Him, labeled "Jews, Turks, Tatars," and below them are the sinners of all ages, murderers, thieves, liars, drunkards, trembling before the Lord in His glory. The river of fire flows across the middle of the wall. Demons appear to be dragging those trying to climb heavenward into the fiery abyss, into the jaws of death itself, while angels are trying to rescue them, pulling them toward God.

I spent a long time admiring this scene and the way it was depicted in such brilliant color. Ionut (pronounced Yo-NOOTS) was, as it turned out, a seminarian, who knew the theology behind the fresco and also the history of each monastery very well.

From Voronet (pronounced Vo-ro-NETS) we continued to the famous monasteries of Sucevita and Moldovita (TSOO-che-VITS-ah and MOL-do-VITS-ah), and then Ionut suggest we add Putna to our itinerary.

"Putna is not one of the painted monasteries, but it is the burial place of Prince Stefan cel Mare, who built all of these amazing churches."

"Why did he build so many?" I asked.

"Every time the Turks tried to invade his realm and his armies repulsed them, Prince Stefan built another monastery to commemorate his victory and as a place where those who died defending Bukovina could be remembered and their souls prayed for, forever."

"So these five-hundred-year-old monasteries are also, in a sense, war memorials."

"Yes. Putna was never frescoed, but it is a very beautiful place, close to the Ukrainian border, and we have plenty of time to visit there before sunset."

"Okay! Let's go!"

At the gates of Putna, the monastery had a gift shop, in which I found a splendid set of embroidered priests' vestments. In order to purchase them, I had to ask Ionut for my money back, explaining that I had more cash for him at the hotel, whereas the monks were not equipped to take foreign checks or credit cards. The blue-on-white cotton vestments are still my favorite liturgical attire during the summer and remind me always of this visit to Putna. We prayed at the tomb of Stefan cel Mare (literally "the glorious"), who succeeded in defending his country's independence and protecting Europe from Turkish/Muslim invasion for so many decades. Western Europeans often fail to recognize the sacrifice that Balkan peoples—especially Serbs and Romanians—have made to prevent the Turkish or Tatar conquest of Europe.

Suceava

At the end of a wonderful day, Ionut and I exchanged addresses, and I gave him some Alaskan souvenirs. From that time on he wrote rather faithfully, informing me that he had found a wonderful woman named Ramona at the seminary in Constanta, on the Black Sea, and he hoped to marry her. The next summer, when my wife and sister and I visited him, he asked Xenia and me to return the following summer to be their best man and matron of honor at their wedding. We agreed.

We planned and saved for our third trip to Romania until, at Christmas, we got word that the engagement was off. Ramona's father was totally opposed to his daughter marrying a man from Bukovina. He might take her there, and then she would live too far from her family. Ramona's father had already bought the adjoining farm, and his plan was for her and her husband to live there, right next door. Marrying a future priest from the far northeast of the country was out of the question. Pressured by her father, Ramona regretfully broke the engagement.

We decided to go to Romania anyway and spent a wonderful week with Ionut, traveling around the heart of the country to major tourist attractions like Brasov and "Dracula's Castle" and again to Mamaia, the seaside resort on the Black Sea.

Upon returning home, we got a joyful letter from Ionut telling us the wedding was back on! George, Ramona's dad, had finally met Ionut (at Ramona's brother's wedding) and liked him. "Okay! Even if you take my daughter all the way to Bukovina, you can marry her!"

So we returned the next year for the weddings—yes, plural, there were two. The civil ceremony, still required by Romanian law, was followed by a village celebration with washtubs full of *holutsi* (cabbage rolls), piles of meats, breads, and fruits. There was lots of *souica* (plum brandy), a violin-dominated band, and dancing in the streets all night long. The church ceremony was in Suceava, Ionut's hometown, followed by an equally lavish banquet and celebration in a downtown hotel.

Ionut was ordained and assigned to a parish, so when I returned for my next visit, we drove into Ukraine and visited my relatives in Pidruda, then drove to Szczawno, where we celebrated Liturgy together, and then to Presov. On the way back to Romania, Father Ionut asked, "Do you think Archbishop Nathaniel in North America needs priests who speak both Romanian and English?"

"I don't know, but I can ask. My brother is his chancellor, so he can tell us. But wait! Are you interested in leaving Romania and going to North America? What would George, your father-in-law, say?"

Much to my surprise and delight, Father Ionut answered, "It was George's idea!"

It took a year or more of applications and paperwork, but Father Ionut and Preoteasa (priest's wife) Ramona-Elena moved to Regina, Saskatchewan. There they revived the oldest Romanian Orthodox community in Canada. By the time they were ready to return home to Europe, Father Ionut was respected and admired enough by the church that the archbishop was reluctant to lose him. He offered him instead a wonderful parish in Kitchener, Ontario. Their sons were born in different parts of Canada. It seems they are going to remain there happily for some years to come, vacationing in Romania and visiting friends and relatives to maintain close ties with their homeland. Most of the family has come to visit them too, except George. If Bukovina was too far, it seems North America is out of the question.

I have asked Father Ionut why it took so long for his father to find him on that first day we met. He remembers very well—he was not scheduled to be my tour guide that day. Their father had first asked his sister Oana to serve as my interpreter on that trip to the painted monasteries, but when Dimitrie came to her apartment, he found that she had the flu and could not possibly spend the day driving around the countryside. So Dad needed to find his son, who, while not as fluent in English, actually knew the churches and their histories much better. We are very thankful for this short illness—Father Ionut and I refer to it as *sfanta grippa,* holy flu. Without it, our relationship and most of his career and life would almost certainly have developed along very different lines.

Coincidence? Accident?

Or is there a plan, a purpose we could not have imagined, at work in our lives?

✠ NINE ✠

Time Out!

PEOPLE EXPERIENCE and deal with time in very different ways around the world.

I spent a year in Russia on sabbatical. The first few weeks my sons and I spent in Moscow, we were housed in a large dormitory room on the grounds of St. Nicholas Church, which was quite near the Paveletsky metro station. My wife was scheduled to join us in a few weeks, and we were eager to find more spacious and appropriate accommodations before she arrived.

One morning, the dean's secretary informed me that they thought they had found suitable lodging for us at an affordable price.

"The lady who can rent this one-bedroom flat to you lives at the end of the Purple Line, near the Sheremetrova Park."

She pulled out a map of the incredibly efficient subway system for which Moscow is justifiably famous.

"You see, here," she indicated with her finger, "in the extreme southeast end of the metro system."

"Yes! This would be great. Can we visit the building and explore the neighborhood?"

"Of course!" she replied. "Why don't we plan to go there tomorrow? I can meet you at the metro station, and we can go together."

"Excellent! What time should we plan to leave? From what metro station?"

She again pointed to the map and showed me the Paveletsky Station. "We can board here and go out to the Vykhino Station, at the end of the Purple Line. Let's plan for eleven AM."

"Fine," I agreed. "I'll see you then tomorrow at eleven."

Now, I teach cross-cultural communications at the university, and I have produced several PBS television programs on this topic. The first basic principle is, "Miscommunication will happen." This is an axiom. A speaker cannot ever say totally, completely, and accurately what he or she means. Some portion of the communication must be inferred or implied. And even if the speaker could say explicitly and fully what he or she means, the listener would unavoidably and predictably miss at least some of what the speaker intended to convey.

Nevertheless, I assumed that we were both on the same

page: meet at eleven AM the next day at the Paveletsky metro, then continue out to the end of the Purple Line.

But when my sons and I arrived at the Paveletsky Station—at 10:30 AM, since we had not synchronized our watches—we waited for a full hour without spotting the secretary. It is, after all, a huge underground complex, and it was certainly possible that we had missed each other among the thousands of riders who swarm into every Moscow train each morning. Or perhaps some unforeseen incident, an unannounced visitor, a summons from a high-ranking official, had required the dean and his secretary to appear elsewhere. Any number of explanations could be offered. The St. Tikhon Institute was a busy place.

"Let's go out to Vykhino and explore the neighborhood," I suggested. "We can at least see if there are parks, stores, shopping opportunities, and restaurants, even if we won't have any idea where our possible apartment might be located."

My sons agreed, and we boarded the train on the Purple Line and rode to its final stop.

We spent the day walking through parks, visiting the open *rynok* (what we might call a farmers' market in the US) and the main grocery store, ate lunch at a Turkish sidewalk concession, and late that evening, after six or seven hours in the neighborhood, returned to the Vykhino Station.

We were about to enter the northbound train to return to the center of the city when one of my sons spotted the secretary, sitting across the tracks from us, on a bench outside the entry. At the same moment, she recognized us.

"I was about to give up on you!" she exclaimed.

"You mean you have been waiting here since eleven this morning?" I asked, incredulous.

"Well, yes. I thought we had agreed to meet here at that time."

"I understood that we were going to travel here together and begin our journey back in town."

"Well, that doesn't matter now. Let's go see this apartment!"

And off we went, using the trolley to get to the tall Soviet-era complex. Our future landlady greeted us warmly and escorted us into the kitchen, where the lunch she had prepared ten hours earlier awaited.

There were no further questions or repercussions. We rented the place for three hundred dollars a month and stayed till the following May. I was simply amazed at the extraordinary patience these Russian ladies exhibited on that day. I doubt I would wait for anyone more than a half-hour beyond the mutually accepted appointment time. They had waited the entire day!

Anglo-Saxon and Germanic peoples see time as a valuable invisible commodity that should not be wasted. This means not being late for appointments, because those who have had to wait will have wasted a lot of time just waiting. Wasting someone's time is theft of a valuable and limited treasure, which is draining away like sand in an hourglass. Late is rude. Late is inconsiderate. Late is actually sinful. People go to hell for late! If you know you are going to be late, it's better to cancel the appointment completely.

I was raised in an immigrant neighborhood populated mostly by descendants of people from western Germany. They were never late. They came early for all engagements and, even for social events, came before the appointed hour. They knew that hosts prepared meals on a tight and exacting schedule. They expected their friends to arrive early so the dinner could start on time, and the cook would have done a lot of mathematical computation to determine when each course of the meal would be served. The party was orchestrated with precise military strategy and would end on time, as the invitation often indicated. If you ever visit Germany, Austria, or Switzerland, you can easily see this determination to maintain schedules and do things in an orderly and punctual fashion.

In Russia, and in many regions of the world, the basic assumption is that most gatherings have their glitches, that the hosts always need a little extra time to prepare. Showing up at the precise published time for any event is a bit rude. Give hosts a little extra time to get ready. They'll appreciate your sensitivity and courtesy.

I once appeared at a colleague's apartment in Moscow at exactly the time he said the party would start. I was happy to have arrived, in the Germanic sense, on time. But the host opened his door in complete disarray, apron splattered, sweating, hair disheveled, and in no way ready to host a fancy sit-down dinner.

I had to ask, "The dinner is tonight, right?"

"Oh, yes! Yes, please come in!"

But, in fact, we were much too early. Escorted to a holding area with plenty of snacks and beverages, my wife and I waited for the next couple to arrive. But the doorbell did not ring for another hour and twenty minutes! The dinner did not start for more than two hours after we got there.

In Germany, when they say eight PM, they mean, "No later than eight." In Russia, eight PM means, "I am having a kind of open house at my apartment beginning at eight o'clock, and I hope you can drop by and join us any time *after* eight." Put this way, would you show up at 7:55? Of course not!

In Russia, this more relaxed attitude toward time is often paired with a remarkable personal piety. I encountered one particularly striking example in Moscow, while I was participating in a commemorative procession dedicated to the Vladimirskaya icon of the Theotokos. We walked from the Dormition Cathedral inside the Kremlin through Red Square, then eastward toward the Stretennaya Monastery, marking the place where the people of Moscow first met the icon and escorted it into the city.

It rained in buckets that day. Viewed from above, the

dozens of bishops, hundreds of priests, and thousands of believers participating in the procession would have looked like a long black snake winding through the narrow ancient streets, everyone huddled under their own or a companion's umbrella. In the center of the parade, I did not need an umbrella of my own—it was like walking under a tent. Beneath our feet, however, there were many missing cobblestones that had become rectangular mud pools, deep enough to cover one's foot completely.

I was carrying a replica of the Vladimir Mother of God icon, depicted as being held or venerated by the metropolitans and patriarchs of Moscow, and the ladies on both sides of me asked if they could hold their candles in front of me. This required them to walk sideways, but it allowed me to hear their continuous singing in honor of the Most Holy Virgin.

Periodically our procession through the narrow cobblestone streets of Moscow had to stop as the police allowed traffic from the side streets to flow across our path. On one of these stops, the feet of the lady next to me disappeared into one of those muddy potholes. Her friends urged her to step aside, but she refused. Mercifully, the crowd surged forward for another hundred yards. As we came to another stop, huddled under our umbrellas, this same woman's feet disappeared once more. Again her friends tried to persuade her to squeeze sideways and bring her sandals out of the mire, but again she resisted. The procession moved ahead another two hundred meters and stopped again, and almost predictably, this same woman found herself stepping once more into the cavern of another huge missing cobblestone.

This time I got involved, gesturing to the side and making room for this woman to move there.

"No! NO!" she replied. She was not willing to step out of the puddle onto the wet stone surface of this ancient alley. I tried to argue.

Finally she spoke, and I had to quit my fussing. *"Vsyo na slavu Bogu!"* she insisted—"Everything to the glory of God!"

This emphasis on honoring God with our every action is not unrelated to the way in which Russian culture treats time in everyday life. It is, in fact, evidence of a very important distinction between two different kinds of time, known in Greek as *chronos* and *kairos.*

In the modern Western world, our only experience of time is chronological, the kind of time we measure with clocks and calendars. Like a river, it flows forward, never back, and what is past is forever gone.

The experience of time the Greeks called kairos, however, is alien to most of the modern world. It derives from a concept of time as repeatable. Important events of the past can not only be remembered, but in ritual, they can be made present. A sacred or significant event of the past can be repeated and its original meaning made accessible under special, intentional circumstances.

A clear example of kairos might be the Seder, the Jewish Passover meal, recalling and celebrating the liberation of the Jewish people from Egyptian slavery thousands of years ago. The *Haggadah*, a service book, contains the songs, hymns, texts, and rubrics for conducting the ritual supper. The instructions within it say directly, "Let everyone celebrate this event as if he himself had been brought out of slavery." The intent is to make this ancient historic event contemporary, as if it were happening today.

There is very little room for innovation at a Passover celebration. The menu has been fixed for centuries. The prayers, hymns, and the four questions the youngest son is expected to ask or even chant in the original Hebrew have remained the same for hundreds of years. By eating the same food, singing the same songs, asking the same questions, a Jewish family puts its members in solidarity, in communion, with all other Jewish families, who, that same night, each in their own time zone, eat the same food, sing the same hymns, and ask the same questions in their turn. There is a conscious sense of worldwide unity in performing these ritual acts.

Perhaps more significantly, by eating and singing and praying exactly this way, the household puts itself deliberately in solidarity with all their ancestors, a chain of Seders that goes back to medieval and maybe even ancient times, back to the time of Moses and the first Passover. The ritual makes the past *present*, allowing the present to become more—a night that is different from all other nights, a night of kairos, sacred time.

The concept of sacred or meaningful time survives among many tribal peoples, even if they do not have a special name for it. During Xenia's pregnancies with our four children, she was also entering into a kind of Yup'ik Eskimo kairos. She would get up early each morning, wash, dress, and leave the house. During the summer, this behavior was not unusual. Almost everyone is up and busy early in the months when the sky never becomes completely dark. But when she continued getting up early and leaving during the winter months, exiting into the darkness and cold of a November morning, I felt I had to confront her.

"Where did you go?"

"Out."

"Yes, I know. But why?"

"It's what we do."

I could have asked, "We who?" but I knew. Yup'ik women. Okay. But what should I ask next? I had no idea.

Several months later, I was invited to deliver a graduation speech at a high school on the Yukon River, where the dialect of the Yup'ik language is slightly different. The students knew I had some limited ability to speak their language, so at supper, they began their investigation.

"*Kituusit?*" (Who are you?/What is your name?)

"*Atertayagaq.*" (The Little Drifter, a name my students at

Mount Edgecumbe High School had given me years before.)

"*Camiunguusit?*" (What village do you come from?)

"*Aipaqa Kuigglugmiunguuq.*" (My wife is from Kwethluk.)

"*Naken Anellruusit?*" (From where did you exit?)

Now this stumped me, a classic example of cross-cultural communication breakdown. Where did I come out? Most recently, the dormitory!

"*Inarvigmek.*" (From the place where you lie down.)

They looked at each other and shook their heads. Clearly my answer did not fit any of the possible options.

"*Camek?*" (What?)

More slowly, they repeated, "*Naken Anellruusit?*"

Oh! "*Tengsuutemek!*" (I came from the airplane!)

Their faces communicated their frustration. Another wrong answer. I surrendered.

"*Taringesciigaatamci.*" (I can't understand you guys.)

"Where were you *born?*"

This triggered an association with my wife's behavior, leaving the house every morning during pregnancy. I went home with some new questions.

I told my wife about my conversation with the high school students. "I had the idea that going out and being born was the same action."

"Yeah," Xenia admitted. "That's true."

"So is there something about how you go out when you get up early and leave the house that is important?"

She looked at me, puzzled, as if she couldn't believe I didn't already know all this.

"Of course!" she exclaimed.

"So what is it?"

"An expectant mother leaves the house, passing through the doorway, always headfirst and never stopping in the passage."

Of course! The old houses, if you looked at them in cross-section, were built in a circular shape with a tunnel entrance. Passing out head first through that entry represented and almost duplicated birth, the child emerging from the womb. A pregnant woman enacts birth, a kind of prenatal education for the child: *Look, baby, this is how to do it, please! Come out headfirst, and do it directly! No stopping!*

My wife was enacting this ritual. It only took a few minutes each morning. She learned this behavior from her mother and others of that older generation. And where did they learn it? From their mothers and grandmothers, of course. And they learned it from theirs—all the way back to, as it's believed among traditional people, the First Mother. Yup'ik women have been doing this since the Beginning, a very long time.

By repeating this behavior, a mother-to-be puts herself not only in solidarity with all other expectant mothers, her contemporaries, but also in continuity and harmony with all her ancestors. Doing this makes her a member of that community, passing this meaningful behavior on, keeping it going for another generation. And she will pass this on to her own daughters, so that each morning during their own pregnancies, they will consciously and deliberately participate in a ritual act that will be meaningful, distinct from all the meaningless chores and responsibilities the rest of the day may bring. It might not last very long, but the time spent going through the doorway "headfirst and without stopping" is also a moment of kairos.

Tribal peoples around the world try to live in kairos as much as possible, so their lives become a sequence of ritual actions, all of which put them in solidarity with each other and their ancestors. And when someone proposes a more efficient method for accomplishing the same task, they are likely to reject the suggestion. It might save time (chronos), but it would deprive them of their moment of meaningful time (kairos).

Kairos requires a significant reality, revealed at some past time, which is of such sacred importance that it can be encountered again and again in the present. Not every present is adequate for this—not all eating and drinking, not all bread and wine, are the same. There must be a qualitative break with the ordinary, when we deliberately leave chronos and say it is time for kairos—time to enter meaningful, sacred time. This is what the deacon says to the celebrant at the start of the liturgy—in Greek, *"Kairos estin."* It is kairos.

The kairos of our worship is most clearly evident in the

Eucharist. Much like the Seder, the Eucharist is based upon a past event, that famous Last Supper in the Upper Room. Certain food was eaten, certain prayers said, certain important sacred words uttered. And for millennia now, Christians have gathered at similar tables, around the same or similar food, and said the same words. Two thousand years have passed, but all that chronological time and distance cannot prevent the believer from gaining access to that supremely holy event, to the sacred reality that was first revealed there and then.

But while the Liturgy is rooted in sacred events that took place in ancient Palestine, it is essentially a projection into the Kingdom to come. Christian kairos is not only a remembrance of the Mystical Supper in about AD 33, but also a participation in the marriage feast of the Bridegroom, an entrance into the reality of the Second Coming, "that you may eat and drink at My table in My kingdom" (Luke 22:30).

One can understand the beauty, the vestments, icons, incense, and singing, only if one realizes that this kairos is different from all others: it is a remembrance of the future. The holy people depicted on the icons are not portrayed in the style of modern or renaissance Italian paintings, but in their future, resurrected bodies, suffused with light, glowing in the reflected holiness into which they have entered, in communion with God.

If we live only chronologically, we must kill time before

time kills us. The hourglass of chronos will eventually drain completely. Chronos leads inevitably to death.

If we live in kairos, or rather constantly transform the chronos of our lives into kairos by conforming to the image of the Perfect One, doing everything to the glory of God, then these days and years become the time in which we "work out [our] own salvation" (Phil. 2:12), drawing constantly nearer to God with struggle and effort, now and in the kairos of the future, with ecstasy and joy forever.

✠ TEN ✠

Robbed!

DURING MY SABBATICAL year in Russia, I was scammed right on the street, in front of the L'viv train station. A few years later, a pickpocket stole my wallet in Levski, Bulgaria. Someone also stole my passport on a subway train in Milan. I seem to go out of my way to get robbed.

The L'viv heist was the most creative. My sons and I arrived there, intent on visiting the city once called Lemberg, no doubt named for the Lemko population from which my grandparents had come. But we had no sooner disembarked from the train than the boys announced they needed to use the bathroom.

Most public buildings in Ukraine and Russia provide toilet facilities. The matron responsible for cleaning and guarding access to them usually stands in the doorway and expects payment for her services upon arrival. The equivalent of a dime used to suffice. She then dispensed toilet tissue of the stiffest and most uncomfortable sort and allowed entry. Without the tip, no one got into the bathroom.

We had just arrived in Ukraine, and I had no local currency. I had brought a hundred US dollars with me to cover all our expenses for the few days we would be in the country. I had planned to exchange this single bill for a few million Ukrainian *koupony* and live well for our short visit to the region. But I could not offer a hundred-dollar bill to the Guardian of the Water Closet. We had to find a bank quickly.

There was a full-service bank opposite the station. We hurried across the pedestrian square that separated the two buildings, my sons dancing as they went. Halfway across the cobblestone plaza, four or five young Ukrainian men surrounded me.

"You want to change money?"

"Yes. I am going to the bank."

"The exchange rate at the bank is not good. We can give you better. What kind of money do you have?"

"I have one hundred US dollars."

"Excellent! We will give you one million *koupony* for this! The bank will give you only eight hundred and fifty thousand!"

My Ukrainian cousin, who had met us when we arrived, looked at me, and I at him: *Is this legal? Can we/should we do this?* He nodded.

I pulled out my wallet while my sons were leaping and jumping more frantically near the curb.

I removed the hundred-dollar bill from my wallet, and the leader snatched it from my hands. He held it suspiciously up to the sunlight, squinting at the watermark.

Just then a larger and older man in a leather jacket rushed up to us, screaming, "What are you guys doing here in the middle of the street exchanging money?! If you want to change money, go to the bank!"

The guy who had my bill almost threw it at me and the entire group dispersed in six directions, including the guy who had been yelling at me. My cousin, my sons, and I shrugged and proceeded to the bank. I put my bill down in front of the teller, who tossed it back in my direction. My hundred-dollar bill had magically been changed already—into a one-dollar bill!

This was organized dishonesty, a gang that had pounced on the greed of a foreigner to swindle him out of ninety-nine dollars. In a country infamous for corruption, this was a normal business day.

My Bulgarian encounter was, by contrast, an amazing anomaly.

I had never been to Bulgaria, knew no one in the country, and spoke no Bulgarian. But it is an Orthodox country with a tragic and heroic history, so I flew over a week before the conference I was attending in Germany to spend a few days exploring it in a rental car. Once I had done this, as I was leaving on the train from Sophia, I had a pang of regret. Unlike my experience in other countries I had visited, I had spent nearly a week there and not connected with anyone, made no new friends. Everyone had been respectful and polite, but I would leave without having gotten to know anyone very well.

The train left the station and made an immediate stop in what seemed to be the first suburb. Hundreds of passengers filled the compartments, leaving only the external hallway clear. The train compartment was configured much like those on the Hogwarts Express, with two facing benches and a doorway on one side, a window and small utility table on the other. I had a seat on one bench, and I could no longer see the Bulgarian passenger seated opposite me. In front of me were the rear ends of several dozen Bulgarians en route to . . . where? Romania? Would we enjoy each other's company like this for the next fourteen hours? I was suddenly dreading the rest of the day. It was July and hot already at seven AM. How would we survive?

Then salvation seemed to appear on the horizon. A vendor came up the vacant hallway with a cart, selling refreshments. I realized I had about ten dollars' worth of Bulgarian *lev* in my wallet, hidden in my front trouser pocket under my cassock. I decided to buy a bottle of water, just in case all these passengers remained on board for the rest of the day.

Robbed!

Besides, I thought, *I might as well spend my lev here—once we cross into Romania, they will be worthless.*

So I stood up and pushed my cassock drapery aside to reach into my pocket and find my wallet. This was difficult—I had to nudge others aside, pull out my money, and pass it to the vendor, who passed the bottle of water and my change back to me. I still had the equivalent of nine dollars in Bulgarian currency as well as coins. But because of the awkwardness of pushing others aside, I returned my wallet not to its original secure location under my cassock, but to the right cassock pocket, and sat down.

At the next major station, Levski, nearly all the new passengers disembarked. They were traveling only as far as the large factory there, and this was their daily morning commute. I was facing the same Bulgarian passenger I had greeted in Sophia. But all those workers had left behind an increase in temperature. Seventeen bodies at nearly one hundred degrees Fahrenheit tend to warm up a place! So before we lurched forward again after this two-minute stop, I lowered the window. My Bulgarian companion looked up and nodded approval.

But the train did not move. Two, four, six minutes passed, and we remained in the Levski station. Finally, a policeman boarded the train and came into our compartment. He spoke in Bulgarian to the other passenger, but I understood well enough, since the language is close enough to Russian. "Were there any Americans here?" he asked the other guy, who shrugged.

— 107 —

EVERYDAY WONDERS

I interjected, *"Ya Amerikanets!"* (I'm American!) But the policeman reacted as if he did not believe me or my answer was not relevant.

The train did not move.

We sat in the July heat for another five minutes, and several policemen returned and spoke to me directly:

"Hde vashe portfyel?" In Russian, this would mean "Where is your briefcase?"

Since I did not have a briefcase, I answered, *"U menya nyet"* (I don't have one).

They left. Still the train did not move.

Finally a delegation of about ten policemen came again directly to me and asked, *"Hde vashi dengi?"* (Where is your money?)

I stood and realized that my wallet was gone. It had in it ten hundred-dollar bills, the money I was bringing to give to my relatives in Ukraine later this summer—one hundred dollars for each of the ten households. I did not need it for my own expenses—I had another stash of money in a different pocket for that. But the loss of my wallet and credit cards could cause considerable problems later on my journey.

As I stood in shock in the center of that railroad wagon, the police all smiled and nodded. *"My znayimo!"* (We know!)

And then the train did, finally, start to move. We traveled forty miles to the next station, and the police insisted I gather my baggage and follow them to the nearby police station.

When I went in to meet the chief of police, he was waiting for me with a display of wallets on his desk. I spotted mine immediately. After polite introductions, he asked if any of the various wallets before me were my own. "Yes. The black one."

"How do you know that it is yours?"

"Well, it is torn in the same place where mine was, and it's the right color, and I suspect my photo ID and Alaska driver's license are still inside it."

"Okay!" the handsome young chief replied. "The trial will be tomorrow. Report back to this office at seven AM. I suggest you stay nearby. Try the Ritz Hotel across the street."

So I dragged my baggage across the cobblestones to the Ritz and asked if there were rooms available.

There were. How much? Four dollars. Okay!

But I had to present my passport, and the clerk pointed to the sign on the wall. Four dollars was the rate for Bulgarians. For foreigners, there was a special nine-dollar rate. All my change from the water bottle purchase was now spent. There would be no supper that night.

With nothing to do and several hours before dark, I decided to explore the town. I had not walked more than ten minutes before the road turned to mud and abruptly ended in a cow pasture. I could have continued, but who knows what you might find in a Bulgarian field? An angry dog? A confrontational bull? A snake? I decided to return to the Ritz and find some way to pass the time, hungry as I was certain to be.

Just then an elderly white-haired man came out the back door of his house and began picking some tomatoes. He looked up at me and said, *"Vy ni ot suda."* (You are not from here.)

I answered, *"Nyet."*

He continued, *"Vy ot kuda?"* probably thinking I was Russian.

I replied, *"S Alyaski"* (From Alaska).

He got excited. "Alaska! Alaska! I watch Alaska on the Discovery Channel!" Then he added, *"Vy goloden?"* (Are you hungry?) and invited me in for a supper of tomatoes, carrots, bread, and fried eggs, with fruit compote as a welcome refreshing beverage for that hot July afternoon.

Returning to the lobby of the Ritz, I found two officers. They demanded to know who Michael Oleksa was, and when I identified myself, they reminded me, "Seven o'clock! Don't be late!"

So, well before seven, I checked out of the Ritz and returned to the police station, where I was certain the inmates had had a more restful night than I had. The chief's driver put my luggage in the trunk and returned to his driver's position. The chief soon joined us, with me seated behind him. Then an officer escorted a young but large Bulgarian lady in handcuffs and placed her on the seat beside me.

She immediately began sobbing, tears flowing down her cheeks, repeating *"Prostite menya!"* (Forgive me!)

Robbed!

In our system, the victim of a crime seldom meets the perpetrator before any court appearance, and even then they are usually forbidden to discuss the crime. There I was in the back seat of a police car, the siren blaring as we sped at incredible velocity past corn, wheat, and sunflower fields, returning to Levski to testify in court about the previous day's events. I did my best to ignore the pleas from this hysterical lady for the entire forty-mile trip.

At the Levski courthouse, she was led away by a platoon of police, and I was taken into the judge's chambers. A Bulgarian who had worked in London for a few years and spoke very adequate English served as my interpreter.

"Who robbed you?" the judge inquired.

"I don't know," I replied.

"Why don't you know?"

"I was sitting down. Almost everyone else was standing up. I could not see their faces. Only their fannies were in my face."

"When did you notice that your wallet was missing?"

"When the police told me."

"You cannot identify the pickpocket?"

"No. I have no idea who took my wallet."

"All right. Sign here, and here and here. Dismissed!"

I moved out to the lobby and saw that same lady being escorted into the same chambers I had just vacated. She screamed to me from twenty meters away, *"Prostite menya! Prostite menya!"*

EVERYDAY WONDERS

Right behind her, they led a much more suspicious-looking guy, unshaven, unwashed, in tattered clothing—probably a poor young man living on the streets. He too saw me and yelled toward me, *"Prostite menya!"* as he disappeared into the judge's domain.

A half-hour passed. Then the lady emerged, free, without handcuffs, with no police at her sides. She rushed toward me, fell on her knees, and again began exclaiming, "Forgive me! Forgive me!"

I insisted that she rise and told her, "Forgiveness is my business. It is my job to dispense forgiveness. Of course I forgive you."

She then told me the story of what had happened aboard that train the previous morning.

"After you sat down, the guy next to you looked up to see if anyone was watching and saw me looking at him. He put his finger to his lips to signal that I should be quiet. Then he reached into your pocket and slid your wallet out of it, and under his shirt. I said nothing. We left the train together. I did not know this man, but he offered me one hundred US dollars, and I ran gleefully (but foolishly) to the department store next to the train station. He followed me. I tried on a nice blouse and skirt and rushed to buy them as he waited for me.

"But the clerk got suspicious when I tried to pay for my new clothes with so much American money. She stalled at processing my purchase and secretly called the police with the emergency button under her desk. They came and arrested both of us."

This explains why the train was kept in the station so long. Seeing that the money was American, the police began searching the train for any Americans, and when they could not find any, they searched for anyone whose wallet was missing. But the Bulgarian word for "wallet" was the Russian word for "briefcase," so when they asked me, I misunderstood.

Again the woman exclaimed, *"Prostitye menya!"* and fell to her knees, crying.

I insisted she stand and told her not to worry anymore. The court had given her the equivalent of American probation and public service, and now I had to put her at ease. *"Boh prostit!"* (God forgives!)

She rose and added, "You forgive me? Well, then, I must confess one more sin. The clothes I'm wearing, I bought with your money."

Now she was much larger than any woman in my family. I had no use for this skirt and blouse, and besides, I was not going to insist she surrender them to me. *"Podarki,"* I muttered. (Gifts.)

She smiled broadly as the police chief Nikolai exclaimed, "It's time for lunch! Let's go eat!" All four of us left the courthouse, found a nearby sidewalk café, and enjoyed a delicious midday meal as guests of the chief.

"And I will buy dessert!" exclaimed the big Bulgarian lady.

EVERYDAY WONDERS

She purchased ice cream cones for all of us from a sidewalk vendor—probably with the remaining portion of my stolen money.

Nikolai handed me my wallet. It had been retained as evidence, but now that the case was concluded, I could have it back. I drew in a breath and calmed myself before peeking inside to see how much of the original thousand dollars was left. It was all there! In addition to nine hundred in American dollars, there was more than a hundred dollars more in Bulgarian lev. I was astounded. How was it possible to be robbed and have the wallet returned with more money in it than when it had been stolen?

As best I could discern, it seems there was such local and national embarrassment that an Orthodox priest from the US had been the victim of a pickpocket on a Bulgarian train that the evening news had broadcast the scandalous story. The whole country was red-faced, and the local police had taken a collection to replace the money that had been spent. What a country!

A hundred-dollar bill in Bulgaria at that time represented three months' pay. Ten policemen could have gained a real bonus that morning just by emptying the wallet. The chief had the wallet in his exclusive possession for most of that day. If he had taken all the money out of it, no one would have known where it had gone. The judge could have returned the wallet to me without any cash. Who would accuse the

Robbed!

judge of stealing the money? Would I ever have suspected? I wouldn't even have noticed that my wallet was missing until I was far from Levski and never known what happened to it—along with my driver's license, credit cards, and one thousand dollars cash.

"Now we need to go sightseeing!" the chief suggested. "You have had such a bad experience in Bulgaria, we need to provide you with some enjoyment." So off the police car sped, up the mountains to a spectacular monastery perched high on the cliffs, overlooking a magnificent valley below. The Bulgarian lady lit candles and knelt once more, begging forgiveness before God and me. "Enough! Enough!" I had to assure her.

We returned to the police station, to the officers' lounge, where a half-dozen off-duty policemen offered to buy me a beer. One of them was familiar with Alaska's history. "Shelikov! Baranov! Rezanov!" he exclaimed. "We know your history!" Indeed he did—better than most Alaskans!

"We are invited to dinner this evening and should be leaving soon," Nikolai informed me. We drove to another monastery and were warmly welcomed by the abbot. After another fantastic meal, we returned to police headquarters. "Don't bother with the Ritz," Nikolai advised. "You can stay in my office tonight." And so I enjoyed the hospitality of the police chief that final night in Bulgaria, rose early the next morning, and continued my journey northward. Nikolai gave me his address on Gagarin Street and insisted I write to him. "Next time you come, we will all go to Sunny Beach!"

I went to my conference in Hanover, Germany, after which I met my wife and sister in Budapest. They joined me for a trip to Istanbul, followed by a visit to a wonderful women's monastery in Greece, then north by train from Thessaloniki back into Bulgaria.

The sisters had provided us with provisions for our journey, but no beverages. Now, in the heat of August, I knew we would need something to drink during the coming day. At about six AM, I woke my sister to tell her I was getting off the train at the next stop to purchase whatever I could find to keep us hydrated for the next six or eight hours. She nodded and rolled over, returning to sleep. I hurried to the door of our wagon as the train slowed. But when it came to a complete stop and I tried the door, it was locked. Our conductor was nowhere to be seen, so I ventured into the next car. Here, too, the door was locked, but the conductor appeared and asked what I was doing.

"I want to get off the train."

"Why?"

"We need some drinks for the day ahead, and I was hoping to find a vendor nearby."

"This is only a two-minute stop. If you disembark, you will miss the train and be left behind. But I have some cold beer in my cooler. I can sell you a few bottles, if you like."

So I accompanied this conductor to his cabin, paid for the beer, and began walking back to my own wagon. The train lurched forward and began its exit from the station slowly. Then suddenly it abruptly stopped again. Had we hit something? Had there been an accident?

Upon entering my car, I found nearly everyone in an uproar. The wagon had been completely silent, everyone apparently asleep four minutes ago, and now they were shouting and running about. "What is going on here?" I blurted.

"There you are!" my sister shouted.

When the train had started to move, they had panicked, thinking I would be left behind, and someone had urged the conductor to pull the emergency brake.

Now the Bulgarian Railroad Police were boarding the train. They demanded to know who had pulled the brake. It had been the Hungarian conductor, who had no idea what was happening. Somehow he could not be blamed, but someone had to take responsibility. There was a three-hundred–dollar fine for stopping a train unless a life-and-death emergency had arisen. Being left behind did not qualify.

The police decided the whole crisis was my fault and began writing up a lengthy citation, demanding three hundred dollars immediately.

My Bulgarian had not improved in the last month, but I tried to dissuade them. "This is not my fault! I was in the adjoining wagon when the brake was pulled."

"Someone must be cited for stopping the train. You will pay the fine."

"Wait, please. Perhaps you have heard of me? I was the Orthodox priest from America who was robbed—the pickpocket stole my wallet."

The police glanced at each other. "You are *that* priest?" Silently, without saying another word, the officer tore up the citation, and they left the train.

At Christmas, I decided to send Nikolai a greeting card. Because it required international postage, I took it to the village post office to be weighed and have the appropriate stamps affixed. As I presented it to the clerk, she said to me, "Oh, look at this, Father Michael! I see you are sending a card to Bulgaria. What a coincidence. You received one from Bulgaria today as well!" and she handed me an envelope.

It was a Christmas card, and in English. None of my Bulgarian contacts had spoken English. Whoever bought it had gone to some considerable trouble just to find a card in English to send to me. I opened it and found a handwritten greeting inscribed inside the card.

It read, "You probably don't remember me. I am the person who caused you so much trouble in Bulgaria last summer. Please forgive me."

My pickpocket sent me holiday greetings! What a country!

✠ ELEVEN ✠

Matushka Olga Michael

THE LIFE AND DEATH of Matushka Olga Michael, the Yup'ik wife of Archpriest Nicolai O. Michael, characterizes in many ways the traditional ideals of her people and faith.

Olga (Arrsamquq) or Olinka was not a physically impressive or imposing figure. She bore eight children who lived to maturity, delivering several without the assistance of a midwife. Her sons and daughters cannot recall that she ever raised her voice to them—Real People do not shout. With a large family and a husband who often traveled to one of the dozen villages entrusted to his pastoral care, Matushka was always busy, but not only with her own household chores. In addition to sewing Father Nicolai's vestments in the early years and crafting beautiful parkas, boots, and mittens for her children, she was constantly knitting socks or making fur outerwear for others. Hardly a friend or neighbor was without something Matushka had made for them. Parishes hundreds of miles away received unsolicited gifts (traditional Eskimo winter boots, *mukluks*) to sell or raffle for their building fund. All the clergy of the deanery wore gloves or woolen socks Arrsamquq had made for them.

As her children grew up and married, Matushka Olga had more than two dozen grandchildren upon whom to lavish her handcrafted treasures, but she never restricted her generosity to her own relatives. Week after week she prepared the prosphora for the village Liturgy. Her knowledge of services was exceptional. Not many Orthodox today have committed to memory the entire service for a major feast, but Matushka Olga knew the hymns of Palm Sunday, Holy Week, and Pascha in Yup'ik by heart. Whenever a visiting priest entered her house, she hurried to don her scarf and request a blessing.

Increasingly freed from domestic chores as her remaining daughters assumed more of the load, she traveled with her husband to regional conferences, sharing her experience and wisdom with another generation of matushki. She enjoyed visiting other parishes during the Selaaviq (Christmas) season, but she was always glad to return home to Kwethluk. Over the course of her lifetime, the village underwent radical changes. From a circle of small, semi-subterranean sod dwellings, it became a typical Eskimo town with a diesel generator, a grade school and later a high school, a community center, a Head Start program and clinic, and several stores. Public radio and television from Bethel, seventeen miles downriver, brought news and images of the world into every Yup'ik home. Woodstoves gave way to oil, dogsleds to snowmobiles.

Some years before her death, Matushka began to feel weak and ill but refused to concern any family members about her condition. She did not improve, and her daughters noticed her loss of weight. When they finally persuaded her to visit the Bethel hospital, she was sent on to Anchorage. The specialists diagnosed terminal cancer. It was too late, they said. There was nothing they could do.

Matushka Olga received the news without bitterness or emotion and returned home to prepare for the inevitable. Her family resolved that medical science would not have the final word, and two daughters left their bedridden mother for Kodiak, where they offered prayers both at Monk's Lagoon and at the reliquary of St. Herman. Upon their return to Kwethluk, they found their mother's bed empty—she was outside hauling buckets of water from the village well, no doubt to do a load of laundry or perhaps to scrub the kitchen floor.

For nearly a year her condition returned to normal, but by conference time the following August, Matushka was too weak to walk or to stand in church unassisted. Archbishop Gregory awarded her the highest distinction bestowed on laity in the diocese, the Cross of St. Herman, draping the enameled cross with his icon around her neck at the end of the feast-day Liturgy.

Her condition continued to deteriorate over the next several months. She began to prepare for death, instructing her family how to do the things she had always done for them and how to distribute her few material possessions among themselves and her neighbors and friends. She had her wedding gown cleaned and asked to be buried in it. She told her sons and daughters not to grieve for her and expressed regret that she had taken a granddaughter into her home, not because she loved her less, but because she feared the granddaughter might mourn her too deeply. As the end drew near, the grandchildren from distant Mount Edgecumbe boarding school were summoned home. An early winter storm delayed them. By the time they arrived, she was gone.

The day of her death, the village priest brought her Holy Communion. She sat up in bed, crossed her arms across her breast and received the Holy Mysteries, made the sign of the cross, folded her arms again, lay down, and fell asleep in the Lord. It was the kind of death we all request, painless, blameless, and peaceful.

News of her passing spread rapidly across western Alaska. Planeloads of mourners began to arrive as the Panakhida was sung at the house. That night a strong southerly wind blew forcefully and continuously, melting the November snow and river ice. Yup'ik neighbors from nearby villages came to

Kwethluk by boat, something normally impossible at that time of year.

Hundreds of friends from far and near filled the newly constructed church on the extraordinary springlike day of the funeral. Upon exiting the church, the procession was joined by a flock of birds, although by that time of year, all birds have long since flown south. The birds circled overhead and accompanied the coffin to the gravesite. The usually frozen soil had been easy to dig because of the unprecedented thaw. That night, after the memorial meal, the wind began to blow again, the ground refroze, ice covered the river, and winter returned. It was as if the earth itself had opened to receive this woman. The cosmos still cooperates and participates in the worship the Real People offer to God.

I included this story in my book *Orthodox Alaska: A Theology of Mission*. Then, in the summer of 1994, I received a letter from a woman in Ossining, New York, explaining that she was not an Orthodox Christian but a woman seeking counseling and emotional support from the wife of an Orthodox priest. When at home, in a sort of vision or dream, she explained, she had encountered the Virgin Mary in a birch forest. The Theotokos walked past her and gestured that she should follow the woman behind her, who walked ahead, out of the trees, and into a clearing. In the center of this meadow was a small hill, but much to her amazement, on the far side was a door. She followed the woman into the "hill house," as she called it, whose interior was illuminated by stone bowl lamps filled with oil and small burning wicks. Signaled to lie down, she relaxed on a bed of moss, and the woman began gently to touch her, as if she were about to give birth (although she was not pregnant). She felt the darkness and pain of years of physical and emotional abuse leave her body.

The woman then lifted her to her feet and led her outside, where a small fire and a large kettle awaited. They drank "tundra" or "Labrador" tea, and the northern lights began a brilliant and colorful display in the arctic sky. The woman then at last spoke, pointing to the heavens: "This is a sign from God of His ability to create great beauty where there had been only darkness and desolation." With this the woman began to walk away.

"Who are you?" the lady shouted, to which the woman muttered, "something Olga." The vision ended.

This lady brought news of this mysterious encounter to her therapist, asking if there was a St. Olga in the Orthodox tradition. Yes, there is, she was told, and she set out to find her icon. Finding the face of St. Olga, princess of Kiev, the lady insisted that this was not the same Olga she had encountered in her dream.

"Could you have met Matushka Olga?" her therapist asked.

"Yes, that's it! What's a 'matushka'?" the lady replied.

Her therapist, as it happens, had recently been reading

Orthodox Alaska, so she made the connection and explained. The lady wrote to me, asking for a photo of Matushka Olga Michael.

This letter came to me on the eve of my departure to Moscow for sabbatical, and I had no chance to rummage through my many photo albums to locate one of the several pictures I certainly had of Matushka Olga. I left for Russia without responding to this request.

The lady did not await my return but wrote to "the Michael Family, Kwethluk, AK 99621," hoping to procure a photograph of Matushka Olga in order to make a positive identification. Matushka Olga's youngest son was then the postmaster of the village, and he handed the letter to one of his sisters when she came to retrieve her mail. This daughter had no idea what the letter from faraway New York might contain. She read the letter containing the details of the lady's mystical encounter with Matushka once, and she was amazed. She read it again. She sat down and read it a third time—and suddenly her house was filled with the sweet fragrance of incense.

Startled, she returned the letter to its envelope and walked over to her older brother's house. He was not home, but his wife was. She asked the wife to read the letter and give it to her husband, then returned home. The sister-in-law read the letter once and found it amazing. She sat down and read it again, and then a third time. She also began to smell the sweetness of incense around her but said nothing as her husband entered the house. She handed him the letter and returned to her job. The husband also read the letter several times. He went to visit an elderly shut-in a short distance away, who teased him with an unusual greeting—"Is that some new kind of perfume you're wearing, or did you just come from visiting a new girlfriend?"

The family decided to send the lady in New York a picture of their mother in which she appeared with other Yup'ik elders. When the photo arrived, the lady exclaimed, "That's the woman I saw, but when I met her she was younger!"

This lady has come to Alaska, studied iconography at Kodiak, and painted several icons of Matushka Olga.

Some years later, during the annual Selaaviq celebration, carol singers, led by the traditional "Star," came to this same elder son's house and sang most of their repertoire, then sat down to enjoy a banquet, ten adults at a time until everyone had had a chance to eat their fill. After several hours, the carolers left, and another relative was reviewing the digital photos she had taken during the celebration. Although no one had seen her during the feast, Matushka Olga's face appeared in the photos, overlooking the gathering. The wall behind her shone with a golden glow, so that others who saw the picture assumed there were ornaments or lights installed on it. But there were no decorations there—the wall radiated a golden light from the presence of Matushka Olga.

Later, it was discovered that this amazing photo was taken with a camera owned by one of Matushka Olga's grandsons, a young man who, with the breakup of his first serious romantic relationship, felt so depressed as to be suicidal. The appearance of his departed grandmother, whom he had never known as a child, reassured him that she was watching over him and gave him new courage and hope. Years later, when he was happily married, he related to others how his grandmother had intervened and probably saved him from self-destruction.

Several young women in Victoria, British Columbia, tragically miscarried in one summer, and the entire parish fell into deep sorrow with the loss of so many infants. Their pastor introduced them to Matushka Olga, and they began to pray daily for her intercessions on their behalf. The following year all of them gave birth to healthy babies.

More recently, a Yup'ik couple with several children decided to separate, primarily because the husband had been smoking pot and drinking to excess. His wife had demanded he stop or go to live with his parents near Anchorage. She and the children returned to her own village in the Kuskokwim Delta. There she sought prayerful support from the local clergy, who prayed with her to Matushka Olga for her intercessions and guidance.

Simultaneously, hundreds of miles away, her husband was sitting in his parents' apartment when suddenly Matushka Olga and her husband, Father Nicolai, appeared. The younger man did not recognize them, but his parents knew immediately who their visitors were. Matushka spoke, saying simply, "We have come to help you!" The couple walked into an adjoining room and disappeared.

"Who was that?" the young husband asked. His parents told him they were Arrsamquq and Uliggaq, and he called his wife.

"When did this happen?" she asked. And they realized that the appearance of Matushka and Father had happened at exactly the time the wife and deacon were praying for their help.

When His Beatitude Jonah came to Kwethluk, he served a memorial service at the grave of Matushka Olga, after which, because of the light drizzle, the people crowded into the small cemetery church for the final blessing. On reviewing the photos taken on that occasion, it is obvious that the altar area on the eastern side of the chapel is aglow with a golden light, not visible when the service was ending but clearly present in the digital pictures afterward. It was the same golden glow with which the house had been illumined previously at Christmas.

A Yup'ik woman from the village of Koliganek, on the Nushagak River, reports that when she was in the hospital, about to undergo brain surgery and understandably apprehensive about the procedure, Matushka Olga (whom she recognized from her icon) appeared to her to encourage and support her. All her anxiety about the operation left her, and her recovery afterward was complete. Her sister, having given birth to a premature, two-pound infant, also encountered Matushka Olga as a vendor selling homemade baked goods in the hallway of the hospital. Later she realized whom she had met, but the lady had disappeared. The child survived and is now a healthy and normal young boy.

Certainly there are more incidents confirming Matushka Olga's favor with God, her sanctity, and the power of her intercessions. We can only hope that she will soon be officially glorified by the Church. The Diocese of Canada has already published an akathist in her honor. Several icons of her are available online, and in St. Nicholas Church in Portland, Oregon, her fresco already appears on the north wall in the nave. Hundreds of women, especially those who have suffered physical, emotional, or sexual abuse, have found comfort and strength in invoking Matushka Olga's presence, seeking her loving and prayerful support. We can only exclaim with them, "Holy Mother Olga, pray to God for us."

✠ TWELVE ✠

The Blessings of Theophany

THEOPHANY HAS ALWAYS BEEN a favorite feast of mine, and in Alaska it takes on a special significance. In addition to the vast amounts of water, snow, and ice present at ground level, southeast Alaska is a rainforest. If you don't like rain, you probably won't enjoy living there. As Richard Nelson wrote in his award-winning book *The Island Within*, rain makes this beautiful landscape what it is, and living things are made mostly of water. We are people made out of rain.

Early in the twenty-first century, the world's largest wild salmon fishery, Bristol Bay, was threatened by the development of the Pebble Project, a British and Canadian partnership that intended to extract gold, copper, and molybdenum from a deposit at the headwaters of the Kvichak drainage, near Alaska's largest lake, Iliamna. While promising roads and pipelines, jobs and investments, the mine also constituted a threat to the pure waters on which millions of salmon depended. Besides this, the process by which the valuable minerals would be separated and milled required the use of deadly cyanide, and the contaminated waste would be stored in "mixing ponds"—forever. Any spill or leak from these would ruin the fishery, also forever.

The dozens of Alaska Native villages downstream became alarmed. If the permits to build the mine were granted, it was highly probable that their economic base and their traditional cultures would be undermined. The Orthodox Diocese of Alaska unanimously passed a resolution invoking God's blessing on any development that would enhance the lives of our people, but refusing such a blessing on any project that threatened to pollute the waters we consider sacred. As we have invoked God's blessing on those lakes and rivers time and again in honor of Christ's Baptism, it would be a sacrilege to allow them to be poisoned. And even a slight trace of copper would be deadly to salmon, let alone cyanide.

There were many citizens' groups downstream that were alarmed and totally opposed to the Pebble Project, but they had no experience in opposing a huge multinational consortium. Fortunately, they were joined by fishing-lodge owners and one wealthy resident whose home lay near the proposed mine. With the financial and legal backing of these astute and committed residents, several initiatives were placed before the citizens of the borough, the region, and the entire state. It was a David-and-Goliath struggle, with the corporate investors far wealthier and more powerful than the alliance of fishermen and local citizens.

Nearly all the communities threatened by the mine were predominantly Orthodox. The Church's resolution needed to be highlighted by media coverage. Filming a few commercial spots for broadcast around the state was easy. Bringing the plight of the local people to the attention of a wider audience would require some investment of time, energy, and resources.

Mr. Robert Gillam offered the use of one of his airplanes and a pilot to transport the temporary administrator of the diocese, Archbishop Benjamin of San Francisco, to perform the Great Blessing of Water in several of the threatened villages. It was one of my duties to arrange this visit.

I explained to the archbishop that this series of visits required considerable logistical preparation. The rivers in western Alaska freeze every winter, the ice so thick that cars and trucks drive on it as if it were a paved highway. At Theophany, it's difficult to find water in liquid form. Each town would need to know our approximate time of arrival. The faithful would gather in the church while someone drove a truck or snowmobile to the airport, usually some miles from the village, to fetch us. In the meantime, someone would have to go to the river or lake to chop a hole in the ice and remain there to prevent that hole from freezing over while we processed to the blessing site and performed the scripture readings.

The bishop replied, "Hole in the ice!" They don't have frozen rivers in San Francisco.

We managed that January to perform the Great Blessing of Water in several communities downriver from the proposed mine. In Dillingham, over a hundred cars and trucks accompanied us to Lake Aleknagik. Photos of the ceremony appeared in the local newspapers and on the back cover of *Alaska* magazine with the caption, "Someone has to protect the water."

In November 2014, the entire state voted in a referendum that asked the citizens of Alaska if Bristol Bay should be permanently designated as a fisheries reserve, within which all mining would be banned. The proposal was approved, not just by an overall majority of voters but by a majority in every one of the state's 411 precincts. It was virtually a unanimous affirmation that the waters in Bristol Bay are precious to all Alaskans, not just those who live or fish there. Some water is sacred to everyone.

I used to go sometimes to celebrate the Feast of Theophany at the village of Nikolai on the upper reaches of the Kuskokwim, Alaska's second-longest river. This village is unique insofar as they continue to speak their ancestral Athabaskan language and, more than most communities, subsist by hunting, fishing, and gathering. Their beautiful log church is among the most picturesque in the state, and the people are warm and friendly. I love them and their land. The river flows swift and clear past their homes, but in the depths of winter it freezes anyway.

One year, after we had finished the holiday celebrations, I had just returned to the welcome warmth of my host's house when the phone rang. It was a caller from the village of Crooked Creek, several hundred miles downstream.

"Is it true that Father Oleksa is in Nikolai today?"

"Yes. He is here."

"Did he have services there today?"

"Yes, we just finished."

"Did he bless the river?"

"Yes. We all went out on the ice and sang the hymns and read the prayers."

"Good! I'm glad. . . . When will the holy water get to Crooked Creek?"

ONE YEAR I spent Theophany in Ethiopia, and I loved everything about my visit. In Ethiopia, Theophany is a major holiday. Police estimates placed the crowd in Addis Ababa on January 19 at one million people.

The day before, on a wide grassy meadow on the outskirts of the city, we witnessed the Great Blessing of Water at a cruciform pool filled with clear, fresh water. At the end of the pool was a bas-relief of Christ being baptized by John the Forerunner, and out of it streamed three fountains of water, on each side and at the top. The entire Holy Synod of the Ethiopian Orthodox Church, about twenty-five bishops, was on hand for the feast, as well as a delegation of Orthodox leaders from around the world.

At the grand finale of the morning-long ritual, some attendants climbed up the plaster image of Jesus being baptized and attached a hose to the topmost stream. The patriarch then proceeded to bless the crowd of thousands with the hose! It was a remarkable and memorable scene. Pandemonium! The locals rushed forward to receive the holy spray, while the foreign photographers fled in terror, fearing their expensive cameras might get doused.

After the ceremonies, we were seated on chairs within a large tent, oriental carpets under our feet. Harmonic singing and elegant dancing commenced, performed mostly by hundreds of students, robed in their school colors, accompanied by drums and rhythmic use of their staffs. It was an unforgettable, joyful spectacle. At the patriarchal palace that evening, the foreign guests enjoyed a traditional Ethiopian banquet of roasted goat, with the delicious spices and spongey bread for which the local cuisine is famous.

After I retired, I thought I'd need a hobby, some project on which to focus. Influenced in part by these happy memories, I decided on Africa.

The newest Orthodox missions today are not in or near Ethiopia but in sub-Saharan Africa. About a century ago, groups of Ugandan and, later, Kenyan Christians, dissatisfied with the doctrines and colonial alliances of the various Christian denominations operating in their countries, began looking for the original, ancient Church. They discovered Orthodoxy, and eventually they were received into the Patriarchate of Alexandria. Through local initiative, the Church grew and spread, and with the help of Archbishop Makarios III, a seminary was founded in Nairobi. I personally had no knowledge of or connection with this new and vibrant expression of Orthodoxy. My new hobby would be to establish some ties with folks there.

Of course, in the age of the World Wide Web, initiating such contact was not difficult. I used Facebook to locate some Kenyan clergy and soon had dozens of new "friends." However, within a month the number of those continuing any regular contact had shrunk to four. I also connected with two young Orthodox men, an altar server and a seminarian, in Uganda. I had learned from my Nigerian pen pal experience as a teen not to take on too many correspondents. Everything about Africa can be overwhelming.

One of my Ugandan contacts was a young man, nineteen years old, who, as I soon discovered, had been abandoned on the streets of Kampala at the age of thirteen. His Facebook photo showed him as an acolyte, wearing a robe and carrying a smoking censer. He had survived on his own by hauling water to households that lacked plumbing, receiving bowls of rice as his reward. He had not been to school for five years, but his fluency in English was superior to that of many college students I had taught. After a few exchanges, he even greeted me in Yup'ik Eskimo:

"*Kenkamken, Ap'a.*" (I love you, Grandpa.)

"How did you learn that?" I had to ask.

"On the Web," he replied matter-of-factly.

"Where on the Web did you find lessons in Yup'ik grammar and spelling?"

"It wasn't hard."

I learned more about this teen's tragic life. His father had been a violent alcoholic and had beaten him regularly. Being abandoned may have saved his life—he might not have survived subsequent thrashings.

Clearly this intelligent, resourceful street kid needed to get back into school, but he had no place to live, no place to study, no place to sleep. We began attacking these problems and solving them, one by one. About three months into this process I confessed that I wanted to send him a gift. What would he like if I could deliver a package to him from America?

"Shoes," he answered immediately. "Air Jordans!"

I knew that typically rural people everywhere, not only in Africa, went barefoot, as human beings had for millennia. I also perceived that many third-world children wore flip-flops most of their lives, and owning classic Nike footwear was beyond their wildest imagination. So, of course, this smart young man dreamed of not just any shoes, but Air Jordans.

"I would be delighted to provide you with such shoes," I wrote, "but you have no address, no post office box to which I could send them. And I have no confidence that such a parcel would arrive. Some customs official or postal clerk could so easily steal them."

"Yes," he admitted, "it was just a fantasy. There is no way for you to send me anything."

That same week I found myself in Denver, Colorado, visiting my classmate, Father James. We have a tradition of going to a Rockies game whenever I come to town. He works in the triage unit of a mental hospital and must interview some of the nation's most depressed or disturbed people. Our visits to Coors Field provide a counterbalance of happy, healthy baseball fans. "If they don't win, it's a shame"—but for true fans, not a tragedy. Baseball people just love going to the park. No other sport defines scoring as "safe at home."

After the game, Father James commented that I had been to Denver often enough to be familiar with all the local established parishes, but there was a new church north of the city that he thought we should visit. So on Sunday, we drove to St. Luke's Antiochian Orthodox Church, a beautiful structure handsomely situated in the suburbs. The rector welcomed me warmly and invited me to preach. After the service, I was introduced to the community as a native of Pennsylvania who had spent most of his life in Alaska. During the coffee hour, a pleasant young lady by the name of Sue approached me and asked where exactly I had been born. She too was from the Keystone State and wondered if we had grown up anywhere near each other.

We had. She was from a small town not twenty miles from mine. Amazing! What are the chances of us meeting years later in the suburbs of Denver? We chatted about our lives, our families, our memories of Lehigh County, when Susan apologized.

"I'm sorry, Father, but I have to be getting home. I'm packing for a trip."

"Where are you going, may I ask?"

"Uganda."

"Uganda!" I could hardly believe my ears. "Uganda?"

"Yes. Why?"

I told her about my street kid and how I wanted to send him a pair of shoes.

"Do you have room for a pair of Air Jordans in your suitcase?"

"Yes!"

So Father James and I went shoe shopping, found a pair in the appropriate size and a style I thought he would like, and he delivered them to Miss Sue's house. Two weeks later I got a Facebook photo of the two of them together, him wearing the shoes.

Accident? Coincidence? What are the chances of this sort of encounter occurring on any given Sunday, in any given church, anywhere in the world?

This young man's birthday is January 8, two days after the New Calendar Feast of Theophany. I renamed him Theophan, not just because his birthday falls during the celebration of this wonderful, life-giving feast, but in honor of the shoes, named for the river Jordan, which he continues proudly to wear.

The Reverend Dr. Michael James Oleksa was born in Allentown, Pennsylvania, and educated at Georgetown University, St. Vladimir's Seminary, and the Orthodox Theological Faculty of Prague. He has spent nearly a half-century serving as parish priest, seminary dean and chancellor of the Diocese of Alaska, and representative of the Orthodox Church in America to various conferences and consultations of the World Council of Churches. He now resides in retirement in Anchorage with his Yup'ik wife Xenia and continues to teach part time at Alaska Pacific University and North Star Behavioral Hospital.

Ancient Faith Publishing hopes you have enjoyed and benefited from this book. The proceeds from the sales of our books only partially cover the costs of operating our nonprofit ministry—which includes both the work of **Ancient Faith Publishing** and the work of **Ancient Faith Radio**. Your financial support makes it possible to continue this ministry both in print and online. Donations are tax-deductible and can be made at www.ancientfaith.com.

To view our other publications,
please visit our website: **store.ancientfaith.com**.

Bringing you Orthodox Christian music, readings, prayers, teaching, and podcasts 24 hours a day since 2004 at www.ancientfaith.com